Money Pizza Respect

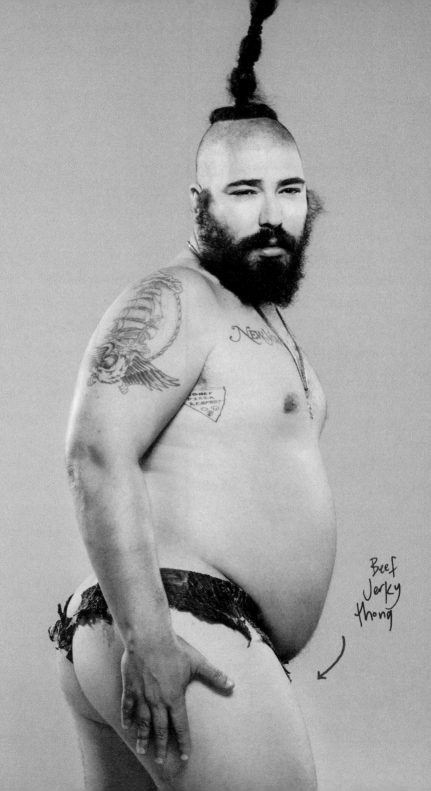

Beef Jerky Thong

# Money

# Pizza

# Respect

Josh

"The Fat Jew"

Ostrovsky

GC

**GRAND CENTRAL**
PUBLISHING

NEW YORK   BOSTON

Grand Central Publishing
Hachette Book Group
1290 Avenue of the Americas
New York, NY 10104
www.HachetteBookGroup.com

Printed in the United States of America

RRD

First edition: November 2015

10 9 8 7 6 5 4 3 2 1

Grand Central Publishing is a division of Hachette Book Group, Inc.

The Grand Central Publishing name and logo is
a trademark of Hachette Book Group, Inc.

The Hachette Speakers Bureau provides a wide range of authors
for speaking events. To find out more, go to www.hachettespeakersbureau.com
or call (866) 376-6591.

The publisher is not responsible for websites (or their content)
that are not owned by the publisher.

Library of Congress Cataloging-in-Publication Data
Ostrovsky, Josh, 1985–
    Money pizza respect / The Fat Jew. — First edition.
        pages cm
    ISBN 978-1-4555-3477-7 (hardcover) — ISBN 978-1-4789-8744-4 (audio download) — ISBN 978-1-4555-3478-4 (ebook)  1. Ostrovsky, Josh, 1985–  2. Actors—United States—Biography.  3. Comedians—United States—Biography.  4. Conduct of life—Humor.  I. Title.
    PN2287.O735A3 2015
    791.4302'8092—dc23
    [B]
                                                                    2015023594

For Monicas

# SUCK MY DICK, JAMES JOYCE. I'M AN AUTHOR NOW.

—Josh "the Fat Jew" Ostrovsky, 2015

CONTENTS

# AUTHOR'S NOTE

Imagine going out and partying HARD. I'm talking binge-drinking and administering drugs through your butthole (they work faster that way). Now imagine waking up the next day in all your clothes, ragingly hungover, in a stranger's house, and someone immediately asks you to recount the events of the previous evening.

You can't. It's simply impossible.

That's kind of like this book. I can't remember a lot of details about what happened to me, so some of the stuff definitely happened, some of it kind of happened, and then some of it absolutely, positively, never happened at all. What can I say; I'm an idiot. Sorry.

So everyone just relax, and don't freak out about the accuracy of every tiny detail. Take it all with a grain of salt. Don't be a dick.

Enjoy!

# FOREWORD

When Fat Jew first asked me to write the foreword to his book, I was humbled and honored. He is a man of many talents and he'd already told me that he'd read one of my books, so he knew what kind of a writer I was. So I felt validated by him asking me, author to author, as well as man to man.

The one thing that everyone needs to know about Fat Jew: He is one funny dude. He will have you laughing out loud within minutes of hanging out. I know a lot of funny guys, but this one really gets me going. That being said, I wasn't exactly sure what kind of book he was going to come at me with. But I was surprised to find that this book is much more of a real memoir than I would have expected. Josh has really put his life out there on the page for all to see. Sure, there are still the hilarious and ridiculous moments that you'd expect from a guy named Fat Jew, but there are also some seriously heart-warming stories about family and relationships as well.

Josh has accomplished a lot of things over the past few years. He is a true businessman in every aspect of the word. He has a social media empire, a very successful wine business, a television career, and now he has written a really impressive book. Like me, he is an "Ideas Man." He is constantly thinking about ways to monetize and brand himself. I can really relate to that. He has an idea, then he immediately starts to figure out how to make it a reality. Ambitious, strong willed, and hungry. All of these traits can describe this funny man, who has the body of a human Shrek, and the hair of a giant adult baby.

I honestly couldn't stop reading this book, and I don't think that you will be able to either.

I'm all about people pursuing their hopes and dreams. Most people are too afraid to reach for the stars. They are afraid that they are going to be burned, and I get that. But when I come across someone who has no fear, who finds the love of god (or whatever you feel like calling it) inside their heart and uses that to create good in this world...I applaud that courage. Fat Jew makes me proud to be an American.

Tyrese Gibson
August 2015

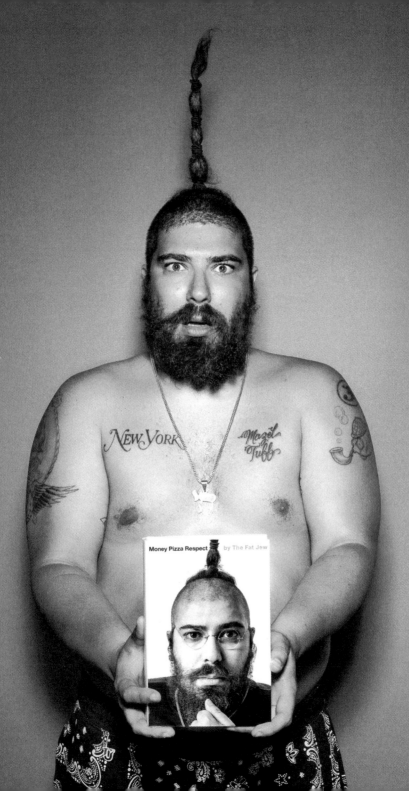

# I GOT A BOOK DEAL/ THE WORLD IS ENDING

## Hahhahahahah I wrote a book.

The fact that I actually wrote a book still amazes me and my mom, and my dad, and pretty much anyone who has ever met me. And it wasn't easy. I slaved over this thing. I started working on it the very day that I got the book deal. Sort of.

I was sitting in the office of my literary agent (hahahahahaha I have a literary agent, why??) waiting to sign the contract for my book. This book. The one you're reading right now, where I compare myself to Steve Jobs on the cover. It was a surreal moment. The fact that someone would actually pay me real dollars to write a book makes me LOL, hard. I sat in my agent's office, staring at a signed photo of him and Bill Clinton, noticing that we've reached a bizarre fucking time in our culture when people like me, who don't really have a legitimate reason to be famous or write a book, are getting amazing opportunities to write books.

"You should be really proud. You really earned this deal. You're really talented," my agent told me.

"I mean, I guess I *kinda* earned it by building up a big audience on social media. But writing a whole book seems like a fucking daunting task."

"You'll be fine. It's not that hard."

That seemed like it was good advice. That's what I pay him the big bucks for. To tell me how great I am.

That night I was getting very pumped. It did feel like all the work I'd been doing for the past few years had been validated. It had paid off.

So I sent out a group text to all of my boys.

> Got a book deal. I'm riiiiiiich now. Meet me at Julius, let's make bad decisions.

The responses from my friends were very typical.

> Fuck you. I hate you. I'll be there in 30

> My mom wrote a book once. It literally won the Pulitzer. But good luck

> Congrats dude. Forget the melting polar ice caps, this is the worst thing to happen to our planet 😈

> They are paying you in money? LOL

> Are you buying the coke? u know u owe me 4 all the years u were poor

Once we were all gathered at Julius (a gay bar for tough gay dudes who watch sports and can kick your ass), I knew I was in for an epic night of drugs and debauchery. My friends are the literal worst, in the best possible way. Once I got four or five whiskeys in me, I began to poll them about what they *really* thought about me being an author. We stepped outside the bar to smoke cigarettes and a joint that was unnecessarily large (like cartoonishly so, but like so big it was mechanically difficult to deal with and ended up being annoying and I wished it was smaller). I guess now would be a good time to explain that that night can be broken down into drug phases. It will help you, the reader, better understand where I was emotionally throughout the evening.

Let's call this

## DRUG PHASE 1 OF THE EVENING:
# WEED VIBES

As we smoked on the corner, my buddies shared some fun ideas for me about how I should go about writing this book. Such as moving to Phoenix, getting addicted to crystal meth, and then writing about that. Or take all the money that I got in the advance and blow it on prostitutes and exotic animals—but mostly on the animals. One friend even suggested that I take the process really seriously, which I thought was hilarious. Then...

"There is no way that you will get this book finished," offered my oldest/richest friend, David.

"A tremendous boost of confidence. Thanks so much for that, you fucking dick."

"What do you want from me? You're obviously smart, but you're also a fucking buffoon who farts in the bathtub and tries to bite the bubbles. Instagramming and making web videos where you get in a Jacuzzi filled with pasta is very, very, very, very, very different than writing a book."

"I guess. Sort of."

"Ummmmmm...Not sort of. Definitely. Writing a funny caption under a picture or a blog post is a lot fucking easier than writing an engaging narrative about your life over the course of three hundred pages or whatever this publisher has you on the hook for."

I got what he was saying, but I also kind of disagreed.

"Writing a caption is not easier than writing a chapter of a book. It's just different," I said, trying to convince myself as much as I was him.

The conversation was making me feel very, very, very not great. *Ungreat.* Could I actually do this? Was I capable of writing a whole fucking book? About my life? Did anyone care? The weed was kicking in and giving me massive anxiety. Or maybe it was my level of drunkenness, or a culmination of all the insecurities I'd had as a child. I started to panic. Paranoia was not my normal weed vibe, but given the pressure I was suddenly putting on myself to write a fucking #1 *New York Times* bestseller, I was feeling trés paranoid.

I had to get out of my head because I was spiraling into a deep hole of depression and self-doubt at warp speed. Which is why I immediately agreed with my boy David, who suggested that we all go this rave in Queens.

Have you ever been to a Pokémon rave? It's fucking *insane.* I had to get somewhere that would relieve me of the weight on my shoulders that was crushing my soul. The Pokémon rave was off the grid in Maspeth, as in, you cannot take the subway to anywhere near there. It's basically thousands of Korean teens taking some form of ecstasy and listening to the most insane techno you can imagine, wearing full Pokémon costumes. Like actually, they take this shit super seriously, which is so Asian. When we arrived we walked into a warehouse and joined the mob of teens gyrating to the loudest EDM (mom, that's electronic dance music) on the entire planet. David handed us each our ration of molly (which, by the way, was wayyyyy too much molly). As soon as it kicked in, my whole world became amazing. My entire perspective on life, the book, my abilities changed in a flash.

## DRUG PHASE 2:
# MOLLY VIBES

"Everything is amazing!!! I got a book deal. I relish that challenge!!" I screamed at my friend Will, who was definitely not listening to me, because he was actually fingering a Korean eighteen-year-old in the middle of the rave over her Pokémon costume pants.

"I'm going to crush this book. People are going to love it. I'm gonna learn so much about myself. I have a great team around me who supports me and loves me. The book will just write itself. *I'm so fucking excited!!!!!*"

There was no response from David, but I really didn't care. I felt like the luckiest man on the planet. For the next few hours I had the best time that anyone has ever had at a Pokémon rave in Maspeth, Queens. I danced, I had an androgynous Asian dressed as Pikachu rub ice on my chest, I told anyone who would listen about how much they were going to love my book (most of them definitely did not speak English) and how it was going to be a long journey for me, but how I was so willing to put in the time and hard work to deliver a book that people would be talking about for years to come.

I really was on top of the world.

Then the molly started to wear off and my emotions became very mixed. (The comedown on molly is way better than on classic '90's ecstasy, but it's still no cakewalk.) All of my friends must have been coming down at the same time, because like magic, we all found our way back to the front door at the exact same time.

"An Uber is going to pick us up in exactly nine minutes and I scored a ton of coke off of this *tranny named Tran!*" screamed David. Yes, a transvestite named Tran. So good.

Fast forward to ten minutes later: In the Uber. The molly is officially done, and now we are all jazzed up on cocaine. I've now shifted from proud and emotional to just very fired up.

## DRUG PHASE 3:
# COKE VIBES

**"Y**ou know what I'm gonna do," I start repeating as we careened down the highway, "I'm gonna go write this book right fucking *now*!!!! Let's do this shit. Like, no time but the present, right? I mean, what if I got like half of this fucking book done tonight? Like what if I just kept writing for like the next twelve hours? Is this insane? I feel like I'm being insane right now, but like good insane, like smart insane."

I had the driver stop at the first pizza place we saw so I could fuel up to write my book. It was four a.m. at this point, and we were all standing on the street eating a slice when it hit me that I needed a title. We tossed around a few ideas:

*Pandering to Millennials*

*Pube Fire*

*I Can't Believe I Got a Book Deal*

*Death of a Salesman*

*The Bible*

*My Mom Fucked Shel Silverstein*

*The Second Cumming*

But then it occurred to me that I have had my title tattooed to my body already:

I've had that tattoo for years. And *Money Pizza Respect* has been my motto for as long as I can remember. It was clear to me that this would be the perfect sentiment for the title of my book. (So either I'm a genius or I'm lazy because I never came up with anything better, obvi.) In my blaze of drug-fueled inspiration, I saw the lights of a pawn shop across the street, shining like a beacon of hope for new American authors. I decided that I would write my entire book on a typewriter, in an attempt to steep myself in the heritage and tradition of these United States.

OK.

This is the moment when my drug plan began to fail (as they always do). This was a fucking pawn shop that was open at four a.m. on a Tuesday. They obviously did not have an old-timey typewriter, because the only pawn shops that are open at this hour are for junkies to pawn stolen watches and electronics for cold, hard smack money. The owner of the shop, who looked like Owen Wilson (but black), showed me this crazy, chunky Gateway desktop computer from 1997. It was perfect. I grew up as a child of the Internet. I'd cut my teeth on a machine just like this one, and now I would be writing a book because I'd made something of myself on the web. There was a karmic and poetic harmony to me finding this exact computer in a pawn shop in Queens. It felt like a real watershed moment for me. Also it was only $74.99. Even while fucked up, I enjoy getting a good deal.

I paid the pawn man, told him that he was now a part of history, and got into a cab with my huge new computer. I was buzzing with literary ideas. Making lists in my head about what stories from my life would make the book.

It was only when I got back to my apartment in Manhattan and started setting up this monster that it occurred to me that it wouldn't be able to connect to the Internet. It was only compatible with dial-up, and I only have wifi, because it's 2015. Then I called Time Warner Cable, which is always to be described as horrible. But trying to figure out if there is some way to get dial-up on this computer, while coked the fuck up at 7:40 in the morning, that is the definition of *hell*.

## DRUG PHASE 4:
# REGRET

I swear I spoke with fourteen thousand Time Warner Cable employees that night, only to fall asleep while on hold with Shaquon, one of the customer service representatives. I woke up at noon, my drool covering the keyboard of the Gateway and Shaquon nowhere to be found. Her shift had probably ended. I hadn't written a word of my book. I felt like death. It was at that moment that I realized I didn't need the Internet to write this book because I was writing in Microsoft Word.

After I showered and ate some egg whites (those undo the ill effects of a drug binge, right?), that computer went straight into the trash. Like I literally threw it into a Dumpster. I couldn't stand the sight of it. I swear on my dead aunt's grave that I didn't write a single word of this book until at least two months later. But that's pretty much par for the course. Whatever. Enjoy the book. Or don't. *Just kidding, please do. I need this book to be popular to pay my fucking rent.*

# 1.

# CHILD ABUSE
(I Know What You're Thinking;
Just Read the Chapter)

Having a kid must be the weirdest thing that can ever happen to you. I don't know what that would feel like, because I don't have kids. It's like, one minute they live inside your testicles, and the next they are speaking English and riding bicycles. My mom just basically lived her whole life in service of me and my brother, which from a young age I always thought was bizarre. From my perspective, she had nothing else going on for her. Like what was she doing for herself? Everyone needs me time. I never really understood why she lived her life like that. *Go to a fucking spa, girl—you deserve it,* I remember thinking, and I still think it to myself. I accepted her life choices, because it was all that I knew, but I didn't get it. I still don't get it. I know we're still at the beginning, but I'm hoping that's the most serious part of this book. Also, starting the first chapter of your whole book with a side note is kind of killer, no?

M y mom always wished she was an actress or performer of some kind, but that never happened for her. I mean, she was in some shitty play in the village when she was like twenty, in which she played a unicorn who was on food stamps. And she got a callback for the Broadway production of *Play It Again, Sam* for a role that Diane Keaton ended up getting. Sorry, Mom. I'm sure you would have been great. But I do feel confident that Diane Keaton was the right choice.

Her only real claim to fame was that she once banged Shel Silverstein in the early seventies, long before she met my dad and started our family. In case you're not familiar, Shel Silverstein was a renowned children's author who was extremely swarthy and legendarily horny. Allegedly, *The Giving Tree* is about my mom's vagina (or

11

so claims my drunk aunt, who told me about their little fling). But besides banging people like Shel, my mom had a normal life and a normal job.

I have a theory that when I was born, she transferred all of her hopes and dreams of being on stage to me. Classic, right? To be fair, I had the exquisite facial structure of an angel, the singing voice of a prepubescent Tony Bennett, and the overall look and vibe of a young Asian woman (look at my headshot). Over the course of my childhood my mom pushed me toward the performing arts. She didn't know any better. It was the eighties. It was back before *Toddlers and Tiaras*, when people finally realized that living vicariously through your children was a bad idea and would inevitably fuck them up. We lived in Brooklyn, and at the age of nine I got my first big break when I landed a real talent agent, named Steve, who wore only turtlenecks and smoked cigarettes in his 1988 Toyota Tercel with the windows closed. Steve would tell me things you don't think people actually say, like "I'm gonna put your name in lights, kid! Make you a star!" I started auditioning for commercials: Coke, Mountain Dew, Skip-It, Jiff, Pop-Tarts, Honey Nut Cheerios. You name it, I auditioned for it. I was pretty into the whole thing, mostly because my mom would pick me up early from school and drive me into Manhattan, where we'd go to McDonald's before each audition and I'd get a Happy Meal. What nine-year-old wouldn't like that? Once we got there, my mom would read the script with me and basically tell me exactly what to say and how to say it.

"Just say it like I'm saying it, Joshy."

"I did. I'm saying it like that."

"No. You didn't. Listen to me. *Mommyyyyyyyyyyy. Can we pleassseeeeee have Pop-Tarts for breakfast again? You know it's my favorite. Even Dad wants a Pop-Tart. Seeeeeeeeee!*"

I did my best to copy her. I honestly have no idea how kids understand what they're saying. Like, how did that kid in *Jerry Maguire* know how to be personable and charming when he was five or whatever? Or Anna Paquin winning a fucking Oscar for her heartbreaking portrayal of a mid-nineteenth-century frontier person in New Zealand? Like, really? I barely knew what my arms and legs were when I was that age.

But after a while I started to get into the swing of it. Soon enough I started getting some callbacks, and after about six months I actually landed my first real job. It was a national network commercial for Hershey's Chocolate Syrup. My parents both seemed so proud of me, like too proud? Like shocked even? But I was fucking stoked. I was going to get to drink chocolate milk all day, and the commercial called for me to wear Rollerblades, which at the time were not even available in stores. I mean, kids knew about them, but nobody—and I mean nobody, not even rich kids whose parents are always in Hong Kong for work—had them yet. Plus, my agent told my mom that I was going to get to keep my new blades. My friends were going to be so jealous. Even at age nine I was deeply concerned about being an early adopter. It always felt shitty to me to be late on some cool shit that other kids were already doing. I wore a fedora and women's jeans to school in third grade because of Indiana Jones, which meant I was basically dressed like Bruno Mars in 2015. I have always been ahead of the curve.

**This is me as a young actor. Seriously. Look at me. Stare at me. I could be wearing a turtleneck made of interracial dicks and it wouldn't be as gay as this shirt.**

The day I shot that commercial my whole outlook on the world changed: There were production assistants waiting on me hand and foot. There was an entire craft services table filled with every variety of junk food, and I was allowed to eat whatever I wanted. People were treating me as if I was better than everyone else, and I liked the way it felt. I was easing into the role of Huge Dickhead

seamlessly and alarmingly quickly. It was like I had been born an awful diva and just needed the tiniest chance to let it out and the second that chance came… *whoosh.* The advertising agency even gave me and my mom two cases of Hershey's Chocolate Syrup to take home at the end of the shoot. I thought I was the most awesome fucking kid on the planet. No one could touch me.

Now that I was a celeb, I expected everyone at my school to treat me like I was Tom Cruise. And you know what the saddest thing is? Once the commercial first aired a month or so later, they actually kind of did treat me differently. And not just the kids, but the teachers and the other parents. I must have been on screen in that commercial for literally three seconds. I rolled by, in the background, wearing bright blue Rollerblades, holding a glass of chocolate milk with a red-and-white striped straw in it. It's super fucked-up how much legitimately better it is to be famous.

Then, about a week after the Hershey commercial aired, I was cast in another commercial, for a clothing company called French Toast. The day of the French Toast shoot, I was a *monster* on set. I was demanding, loud, and shitty to everyone who worked on the crew. I believed deeply that I had earned the right to anything I wanted. I was like Mariah Carey, at the height of her career, but with a tiny little penis.

"Hey, Greg, can you go ahead and get me some McNuggets for lunch?" I yelled to an assistant as I sat in my dressing room. I was *nine.*

Greg looked at me like he had just walked in on me blowing his uncle. He was clearly upset and disturbed.

"Actually, I'm Brian."

My mom, who was sitting in the room with me, gave me a dirty look.

"You don't have to get him anything, Brian. He can eat the catering. Josh, you're being a spoiled brat," my mom stated calmly.

But in the end, I won, because I made Greg/Brian go to McDonald's to pick me up some motherfucking nuggets and one of those sundaes with nuts. I was an instant prima donna, a child asshole of the first order, an overnight sensation who knew he had the goods. Nothing was going to stop me as I skyrocketed to fame, crushing people's spirits all along the way. Not only did I want success and fame for myself, I wanted to ruin other famous kids and adults. I wanted to luxuriously bathe in the tears of their failure. At that age, you really only care about yourself. (Or maybe that's true at all ages.)

After that shoot I was *balling*. Coming back to school the following week, I had a whole new look. Magnetic earring (my parents wouldn't let me get a real one), New York Knicks jacket, Oakley sunglasses, and a Nintendo Power Glove. Yes, I actually wore a Power Glove to school as a fashion statement. It actually had electrical cords hanging from it, and you know what? It was fucking awesome, and I stand by that choice today. The girls were eating it up. The boys wanted to be me. It was incredible. I was the most famous kid in my school. Even more famous than this kid Mark who had been on *America's Funniest Home Videos* because his indoor basketball hoop had fallen on his head. I hated him and enjoyed surpassing him almost more than I enjoyed the fame itself. I was in the big time now. Jamie, the hottest girl in our class (and also the only female who had anything even close to actual boobs), asked me to sit next to her during lunch. I was the *king* of the fourth grade, and I couldn't have *possibly* been taking myself more seriously.

Then, about a month later, shit got really classy when my mom took me to an audition for the Broadway production of Neil Simon's *Lost in Yonkers*. I nailed it. They fucking loved me and asked me to come back the following day for a callback to read with the actor who'd be playing my father. When I showed up for the second audition I was so prepared. I'd memorized the script and I knew exactly how I wanted to do it. I walked into that callback in what felt like slow motion. My confidence was soaring. I was looking fly in my khakis, turtleneck, and tiny gold chain. I was owning my shit.

The actor who'd been cast as the father was in the room already. He was really funny and super nice to me. Turns out that the actor was a relatively unknown Kevin Spacey. When we read the scene, it was like magic. The casting director and the producers were flipping out about how much they loved it. I was sure that I had gotten the job as I walked out that room.

"They loved me, obviously. They thought I was really funny. I'm going to be on the stage. Broadway, baby." I popped open a Sprite and took a sip. "But we both knew I'd get it, am I right, Rebecca?" (Yes, I had actually started calling my mother by her first name.)

We got the call the next morning that I was cast in the play. I was so stoked, but I remember feeling almost vacant, like I had gotten used to this already, like I was a few days away from making an art film because I was bored by the commerce of it all. It had been two weeks.

My parents were freaking out. They couldn't believe that I was going to make my Broadway debut. I did feel totally untouchable, like I'd really made it. I was a star. Three auditions up, three knocked down. *This was my fucking craft.*

I brought this brimming confidence into my next audition, which was for another commercial. My mom picked me up from school in our station wagon and drove me down to the casting offices. As usual we were running late and rushing to get there before it ended. My mom pulled up to the office building, but there was nowhere to park. Driving in New York City is a fucking nightmare, and it has been since the beginning of time.

"Joshy, I'm just going to double park here and come up with you."

"Mom, why don't you just wait here with the car. I'll go up by myself. I know what to do."

"I don't know, Josh. I should go over the lines with you."

"Mom, I got it. I'll be good."

I'd been to this casting office before so I knew the drill. I went upstairs, sat outside the room, and read through my lines a couple of times. It was really easy. I just had three of them, so when they called my name I was ready.

"Hi, I'm Joshua Ostrovsky!" I said as I walked into the room, and I'm pretty sure in hindsight that I was basically singing. It was like I was mad coked-up, but instead of cocaine it was just *extreme* prepubescent confidence and tons of Skittles. The people in the room seemed somber and almost sad. I wasn't sure what was happening, but I didn't know what else to do but keep on dialing up the hammy meter and going more over the top. All I knew how to do was to act *more*.

"Hello, Josh. Just stand on the X and read us the first line," one of the casting people said.

"Suuuuuuuuuuure, *folks*!!!!!" I said. I was being so intense and actor-y.

I looked into the camera and delivered my first line.

"*I fellllllllllll off......my......SKATEBOAAAARD!*" I was essentially singing and doing jazz hands.

"Josh, can we try one of the other lines, maybe?" The casting director seemed confused by my performance.

"Sure, sure." I thought I'd nailed it, so I was a little shocked by the cold response from the people at the casting desk. "Let me try this one...*I tripped DOWN...THE...STAIRS and got bruises on my LEEEEEGS!!!!!!*" With this line I somehow took it even further in a theatrical direction. I added a 360° spin and on the word *legs* slid on my knees toward them like I was in *West Side Story*. I'm not kidding or exaggerating. I pray one day tape of this is unearthed. I was doing full-blown Sondheim up there.

Silence.

Then the director took a deep breath.

"Okay, Joshua...let's—"

I cut him off. "I'm sorry, I'm sorry. No, I get it. Let me try the last line." I turned my back to them. "I was playing *catch* [I turned my head over my shoulder to make eye contact] with my brother [full turn around] and got *hit* with a *baaaaseballllllll!*" I said the last word like Oprah and finished the line by miming a baseball swing, then pretending to watch the ball sail out of the park and taking a gratuitous trot around the "bases," smiling and waving at the "fans" as I rounded the diamond. I did a big finish at home plate, and then, with a shit-eating grin on my face, I went to high-five all of the casting people as if they were my teammates, who all reluctantly and awkwardly obliged. There was so much joy in my heart at that moment.

The room was oddly silent. One of the guys at the casting table looked like he was angry at me. Another woman seemed borderline disgusted. It was all very confusing.

"Josh," one of them said quietly. "This commercial is a public service announcement about child abuse. I think you should go out to the waiting room and go over this with your mom or dad and then come back and try again later. This is a very serious commercial, and it would be best if you tried something different. Okay?"

My eyes filled with tears. I was beside myself. I was an actor, this was my *life*. How could I have blown it so badly? I could barely speak. If I had been wearing a scarf I would have tossed it flippantly around my neck and stormed off camera.

I ran out of the room, out of the casting office, and into the elevator. When I got down to the street my mom was sitting in her car in front of the building. I opened the door.

"You embarrassed me!!!!!!!! I hate you, Mom!!!" I screamed and bawled.

"Oh my God! What happened, Joshy?"

I handed her the piece of paper with the script on it. She started to read it, and I could see in her eyes how bad she felt.

"I was doing it wrong, and they all must be laughing at me up there. I hate this. I'm never going to another audition again."

I cried all the way back to Brooklyn. I was mortified. Was my career over? Had I started from nothing, honed my craft, become a raging asshole diva, peaked, and spiraled out of control, all within the matter of three or four weeks? Yes.

To make matters exponentially worse, the next day we got a message on our answering machine from my agent saying that the producer of *Lost in Yonkers* had decided to offer me the understudy role instead of the actual part. After that turn of events and the child abuse scandal, I was pretty sure that I never wanted to think about acting again. So I told my mom and dad to call my agent and tell him that I quit. I was a washed-up star. I was still nine. It was over. I just wanted to escape. Go somewhere where no one would know my face. Live a quiet life.

"Are you sure that's what you want?" my dad asked.

"Dad, I'm done. I'm gonna focus on sports. I wanna play for the Mets, so I can't really have too many distractions."

And that was it. They never asked me about acting again. My parents never made me do anything I didn't really want to do. I'm not sure that was a good thing, but it's the way I grew up. I didn't ever get to play for the Mets because I'm Jewish and Jewish people are pretty bad at sports. Actually, really bad at sports. When I was growing up we had a book in our house called something like *Jewish Sports Heroes*, and I'm not kidding, it was twelve pages long, just Sandy Koufax, some boxer from 1909 named something like Max Rosensteinwitz, and that was basically it. Remember, Jewish kids, you can be basically anything you want, like literally a fucking astronaut, but you will never be a professional athlete.

# PASSIONATE
# LIAISONS

ere's something you don't know about me: When I was twelve I wanted to write erotic novels. I swear I would have put them in this book if my fucking mom hadn't lost them when she and my dad moved out of New York City. I do distinctly remember one of them being about a teacher named Mrs. Parker who deflowers her male student—a slightly overweight Jewish kid named Mark who moves into Manhattan from somewhere suburban. Mrs. Parker shows Mark the big city and they have a very steamy love scene in the bathroom of the Olive Garden in Times Square. (Just to give you an idea of where my head was at then.)

When I first started thinking about writing a book, this book, I pitched an erotic novel. I'm not kidding. There was still a part of me that needed to express itself via the medium of erotic fiction.

But my agent discouraged me from even bringing this idea up with publishers, and holy shit, was he right! Let's just say that when I did pitch that idea, I did not get a ton of support from editors. I ultimately settled on this publisher, and this book is clearly not an erotic one, but...my agent's assistant read the erotica writing sample I had prepared and she secretly emailed me and told me how "amazing" she thought it was. And how she knew "that once I got some more credibility as an author, I would break out as a star in the erotica genre for my second book." Receiving that email was one of the most rewarding moments of last year. Thank you for believing in me, assistant girl, thank you.

I was very encouraged by her words, and I told my agent and my editor that I would only do this book if they let me throw in at least one erotica chapter. So that is what you are about read. None of the following actually happened, but there are definitely moments that are pulled from true events. Call it erotica, fan fiction, whatever you think best suits it. Or call it trash. But I wrote it for you and I think you will enjoy it.

You're fucking welcome in advance.

# an EROTIC STORY

### BY JOSH OSTROVSKY

I t was the coldest day of the year. The coldest day of his life, maybe. That's how it felt. But he'd grown up in New York and should be used to the cold. He was wearing a blue fleece onesie, hunting boots, and sunglasses. The show started at four, and Josh knew that if he didn't run, he would be late and the whole day would be a wash. This was literally the only thing he'd gotten out of bed for today, which was embarrassing, but it was his life now. Fashion week always seemed ridiculous to him. *Who cares? Why was he invited to all of these fashion shows and parties? Why did he go?*

4:11 p.m.

He ran through the door, got his name checked off a list by a small PR girl (definitely named Rachel or Lauren) in all black holding an iPad, and found his seat. The space was huge and crowded with losers in "cool people" costumes. The show was starting late, as they always did, so he was fine on time. Checking emails on his phone as the lights started to go down, he felt a hand on his knee. The touch was soft, almost comforting, like the person to whom it belonged was an old friend. When he looked up, he saw the familiar face of a chocolate-skinned man staring almost aggressively into his eyes. Kanye West.

"You're the Fat Jew," Kanye said, as if he was explaining it to Josh.

"That is a true statement," Josh replied. That's when he noticed that Kim Kardashian was seated next to her loving husband and was now turned around and half-smiling right at him.

"Come find me after the show. I think we should talk," said Yeezy.

"Okay…"

"I like what you do on Instagram. That shit is real. You're an artist. I get it. And I think you know Svetlana."

Josh did know one Svetlana, a Pilates instructor from the Ukraine from whom he'd taken one session before deciding that Pilates was stupid.

"OK, oh yeah, for sure." Josh said, smiling as loud electronic music came on throughout the lofty space and models began stomping down the runway. Too distracted by what had just happened, Josh barely even realized the fashion show was happening until it was over. He'd spent the entire show trying to sit in as cool a way as possible. Kanye made him nervous. Very nervous. Which was a strange feeling for Josh, because he never felt nervous. *Nervous* was the last word someone would use to describe him.

When the show ended and the waify models had cleared the stage, there was such a flurry of photographers and crowds swarming Kim and Kanye, Josh never even saw them leave. He didn't know what to do, so he decided on standing by the line of cars, assuming that eventually they'd come out to be collected by one of the idling black

SUVs. After two cigarettes of waiting in the freezing cold, he said *fuck it* and headed off. He was a big guy and normally could withstand this weather, but this was just too cold for Josh. Even if it meant missing his chance to bask more in Kanye's presence.

Josh headed to his friend Peter's house, which was around the corner, to see if he was home. He was dying to relay the story to someone, anyone, really. Josh didn't normally get starstruck, but there wasn't a person on this planet that wouldn't be starstruck by Kimye. Unfortunately, Peter wasn't home, so Josh was forced to take refuge from the cold at Starbucks. He just sat there looking at Instagram, dying to tell someone that Kanye knew who he was.

After three skim lattes, a freezing cold walk home, a very satisfying masturbation session, and hot shower, Josh was getting dressed to go to a very swanky cocktail party. He decided to wear black jeans, a tank top with a spray-painted cartoon of the Twin Towers on it, and his denim jacket that had the words *Mazel Tough* embroidered in big letters across the back. To finish off the look he put his hair up into its signature vertical ponytail on the top of his head.

The party was full of more fashion people. His peripheral friend Bee Shaffer had invited him because her mom, Anna Wintour, supposedly thought he was "interesting." It was a small group of people at Anna's brownstone on the Upper East Side. Josh was nursing a Scotch neat and talking to two sisters who owned a jewelry company or something. He wasn't really paying attention.

"We're actually flying to Tulum tomorrow with Karen O and Dave Franco to shoot our lookbook, so you should

definitely come with and hang!" one of the sisters said
to him.

"Oh, shit. Kim and Kanye just walked in. Love that,"
said the other sister, looking past Josh toward the door.

Josh turned around to look and lo and behold, there
they were again, in new outfits. Kim's pencil skirt hugged
the curve of her hips like a second skin. Her face glowed
and her tits were huge and supple, stacked braless beneath
a sheer cream blouse atop her tiny waist and truly
amazing ass. She looked fucking great.

"I gotta pee," Josh said, excusing himself. He walked
toward the door where the Wests were still standing, talking
to Anna and Bee. He'd been thinking about the two of them
ever since. About the way Kanye touched his leg, the way
Kim looked at Josh like she knew something he didn't, the
way she was silent yet entrancing all at once. Josh was never
drawn to anyone the way he was drawn to them.

After he peed and had another drink, Josh found his
way over to the Wests, who were sitting on a dark green
suede couch in a large room filled with huge black-and-
white photographs of Aborigines.

"Yo. The Fat Jewish," Kanye announced.

Josh sat down next to Kanye. Kim was smiling but still
mute.

They talked about Josh's Instagram feed and his
videos. Kanye was a real fan, which was crazy to Josh.
Finally, Kanye put his glass of Champagne down on the
coffee table and looked at Josh, putting his hand on his
leg again. His touch was so gentle. *You are so misunderstood*,
thought Josh.

"I like the way you see shit, because it's nothing like the
way I see shit. You understand that?"

Josh didn't *really* know what he meant or why he might say that, but that didn't matter. "Of course I do," he replied.

"And I make it a point in my life to have contrasting views expressed to me about my work. See, I'm not a rapper, I'm an art student. Kim's a student, too."

Kim nodded.

"Oh…OK," Josh said, his eyes glancing down for a second to Kanye's hand still resting on his thigh. He wondered if Kanye could feel him trembling a little bit.

"So, why don't you come back to the hotel with us, 'cause I have some new shit that I wanna run by you and I'm kinda hopin' you hate it, 'cause that would be very helpful to me."

"Right. Your hotel, OK. Now? I thought you lived here."

"We're in between places, so we're staying at the Pierre."

"True," said Josh. "Aight, I'm down. Now?"

"Yes, now. Unless you're trying to stay here all night. I'm bored as fuck here, and so is Kim," Kanye said, looking around the room. Kim said nothing. She didn't look bored to Josh. She looked like a selfie of Kim Kardashian. They got outta there.

Their hotel room, a suite at the Pierre, was enormous and plush.

"This place is beautiful," Josh remarked when they walked in. Kim walked in and immediately sat down on one of the couches. She put her legs up and sat statuesque like an Olympian goddess.

"The place is all right. Too blue," Kanye replied as he walked toward a stereo system set on an antique credenza across the massive sitting room. He flicked a few switches and a rough, rowdy beat blasted from the speakers. "Now, fuckin' really tell me what you think of this," he shouted at Josh over the loud track, bringing him coconut water that he'd pulled from a small fridge.

"Yeah, yeah, I will," Josh said, nodding cooperatively, taking the coconut water and having a sip.

"OK. Go sit down next to Kim."

He followed Kanye's order and sat right next to her. He could smell her perfume: a crisp scent that was something like clean laundry and roses and mint, all rolled into one intoxicating aroma. His breath grew heavier, and he hoped she wouldn't notice.

Kanye began to rap some of his "new stuff" while Josh and Kim sat listening. Occasionally Kim would do something on the laptop next to her, which, weirdly, was a Dell. Josh couldn't believe it. *Why does Kim Kardashian own a fucking Dell? She has all the money in the world,* Josh thought to himself. He couldn't believe any of what was happening. Then, seamlessly with his rap, Kanye started shouting orders at Josh.

"Take that jacket off, buddy!" he yelled. "Take all that shit off! Yeah, take those fuckin' jeans off! Yes! We're gonna take some fuckin' pictures!"

One thing led to another and soon Josh was sitting stark naked next to Kim, who had slipped out of her dress and stilettos, leaving them in a pile next to the couch. She was completely nude and looked stunning. Her skin was the color of an iced latte. Kanye, with his clothes still on, started snapping photos of Kim and Josh on a camera that looked like it was made in the early 1980s. *Flash! Flash!* Kim ran and grabbed a bottle of lube from a drawer and covered her breasts in the slick stuff. She was rolling around on the floor now, and Josh joined and did the same, their bodies intertwining like soft, slippery eels. More flashes. The music still blasting. Josh had a full-blown boner and was proud of it. He felt like he may have finally found his spirit-sex partners in Kim Kardashian and Kanye West.

"You guys have like the same fuckin' body!" Kanye shouted with glee. He ripped his blousy top off, his body way more chiseled than Josh had imagined. He was actually a beautiful, beautiful man. His pants came off just as fast. Josh and Kim exchanged an approving glance as Kanye's impressive member flopped out of his ripped designer jeans.

Was this really happening? Not in his wildest dreams did Josh ever think he'd be in a hotel room, naked, with two of the most famous people on the planet.

The three of them moved to the bedroom, an equally palatial space, filled with plush powder-blue upholstery and gold-accented antiques. On the bedside table was a small box with more lube, a pirate eye patch, dishwashing gloves, and lots of condoms, different sizes.

Kanye threw on the eye patch and the gloves and found the biggest sized condom in the box. He then threw Josh a regular-sized condom, which Josh slipped on.

"Now you pleasure my wife, funny man." Kanye was smiling.

Josh really had no choice. He started groping Kim gently. Kanye lounged catlike and watched. Josh caressed Kim's supple breasts, taking one out to expose her majestic dime-sized areolas, which he began softly chewing on, like a baby with no teeth on a pacifier. A few minutes in, Kanye joined the sexual debauchery. He sidled up alongside Josh and softly kissed his neck, which was unexpected but certainly not unappreciated. They both began grabbing at Kim, like cheetahs who have run down a helpless antelope. There was so much lube everywhere, everyone was laughing and moaning and the vibes were just fucking right. Josh, ever the sexual deviant, was unsure of the boundaries, unsure how far Kimye was willing to go. He decided to test the waters of his darkest fetishes by putting Kim's entire foot into his mouth. Rather than stop him, she giggled mischievously and began to jam it even further down Josh's throat, while simultaneously pleasuring his member with her soft and flawless Armenian hands. Kanye began clapping with approval, taking immense joy in the sexual rodeo that was unfolding before his eyes. Kanye inserted himself into Kim's mouth and began slowly thrusting, as Josh mounted her, forming a double team that wildly satisfied Kim. As the sweat began to drip and the intensity increased, Kanye slipped into Kim from behind, and for a brief moment, Kanye's balls slapped against Josh's. The two locked eyes, and Kanye reached his hand out for Josh to take, and he did, the two gripping each other while continuing to fuck Kim. The thrusting of bodies intensified, and as the German house music reached a crescendo, all three of them simultaneously climaxed, breathless.

Afterward, Josh lay cozily sandwiched between the Wests, so peaceful that he was almost sleeping.

"You seen *Despicable Me 2*?" Kanye asked, breaking the silence.

"I haven't, but I'd be down to watch it," Josh answered.

"You'd be *down to watch it*?" Kanye spat at Josh, imitating him.

"Um...yeah?"

"Well, thank fuckin' God, 'cause we watchin' it right now."

And with that, Kanye bounced out of bed and slipped a DVD into the player under the TV.

The three of them sat in bed, naked, and watched the movie from start to finish while Kanye narrated every major scene through the entire thing. At some point, sushi was delivered to the room, and it was fucking delicious.

The sun eventually rose and Josh started getting dressed to go. Kanye slept like a sweet child, swaddled in expensive sheets on the far side of the bed. As Josh slowly shut the door to the bedroom, so as not to wake anyone, Kim slid out of bed and ran to him.

"Thanks for last night, Josh," she said. It was the first time he'd heard her actually speak since meeting them at the fashion show.

"You're welcome, Kim. Thank you guys," said Josh.

He took the elevator down and walked through the quiet lobby of the hotel and back out into the cold, back into his life.

The End.

# MY DAD THINKS
# I'M GAY

**Y**ou're not tired. Stop saying that you're tired. It's not even late."

"Yeah, I am, Dad. And yes it is," I pleaded, looking out the window of our minivan at the passing delis—places with names like Rocco's Best NY Gourmet Deli, Lloyd's Gourmet NY Best Deli, and Best NY Gourmet Deli by Andrei. They were all still open, but it was late. Like, eleven p.m. That's fucking late for a thirteen-year-old, especially if he's exhausted because his bar mitzvah party ended less than an hour ago. I had spent the last several hours dancing to "Whoomp! (There It Is)" and having my Jewish aunts with tremendous breasts tell me how proud they are of me, and I just wanted to go to sleep. My dad didn't care: he was on a mission. The objective: to de-gay his maybe-gay son.

The truth is, my hard-ass immigrant father did have very good reason to believe his thirteen-year-old son might be waaaaaay into dick. As a really little kid, I was very into fashion, I made and served Play-Doh hors d'oeuvres, and I was obsessed with disco music. Not to stereotype, but that shit's all pretty gay. Look at me up there in that picture at Jew camp from that year. I'm holding on to that other kid like he's my husband.

The tipping point for my father was the theme I'd picked for my bar mitzvah: autumn. Like the season. You have to understand: My dad was born in Russia, grew up on the streets of Brighton Beach playing stickball with a rock or whatever kids did back then, and got a fake ID so he could work at the post office when he was fourteen. *Fourteen.* He also had a full beard at that age. When I was fourteen I was just discovering that I could make a milky substance come out of my penis, and I had one long pubic hair that was longer than my dick. By that age my dad already had a full-time job, had almost definitely seen two or three men stabbed to death, and knew how to drive stick. He'd never really known a homosexual, so to him, having an autumn bar mitzvah theme instead of, say, basketball or rock music, was super gay. He couldn't even remotely process it. My mom, on the other hand, was thrilled with that choice. Together we'd picked out the decor: Faux leaves were delicately draped throughout the banquet hall, the space was lit in warm autumnal tones like eggplant and ochre, the tablecloths were designed to look like bark, and the table's centerpieces were gigantic cornucopias, each exploding into a sprawl of beautiful fall mélange. Very, very, *very* gay. Like, I could have had bouquets of autumnal-hued cocks knotted together on each table and it wouldn't have been as homosexual as having wicker horns filled with the seasonal fruits and vegetables of a crisp fall harvest.

So I was tired as fuck, being driven by my slightly homophobic dad far from my adorable fall-themed bar mitzvah party. I had no clue where we were going. But the roads seemed familiar.

"Where are we going?"

"Brighton Beach."

"Why, Dad?"

"Because. Stop asking questions."

My dad may have let the bar mitzvah theme happen, but he'd made it super clear that he was not into it—I realized just how much when in the distance I saw a very bright, very neon, very scummy looking strip club.

"When we walk in, I don't want you making a scene."

"Are you sure they'll let me in?"

"No."

"So why the fuck are we going?"

"Language, Josh!"

"Can we please go home? There's leftover cake and I know it's gonna get stale really quick because it was super moist, and generally—"

"You ate enough cake. It's time you start appreciating worlds outside of food, theater camp, and your Walkman."

My dad has always referred to any personal music player as a Walkman, even today with iPods.

"Why?" I asked, genuinely hurt.

"Because you're a man now." He pushed on the gas, speeding through a red light.

"But why?"

"Because that's what happens at a young man's bar mitzvah. He passes over into the next phase of his life."

"But why?"

"No more questions please. We're almost there."

He turned on the radio loud (my dad always listened to AM

news radio at top volume, like it was music) until we pulled into the parking lot of Ivan's Sexy Rodeo and I looked at the glowing green clock in the dashboard: 11:26 p.m. We were welcomed at the door by a scary thin man with one eyeball that was much, much bigger than the other. I tried not to look at his fucked-up face. It reminded me of when I watched *Tales from the Hood* and I got so scared that I threw up on my friend Micah's cat. The guy seemed to know my dad, which also scared me. A lot of things were scaring me. Like the overwhelmingly pungent smell of vanilla, sweat, and soy sauce when we first walked in. But I was a man, I guess, so I tried to act like one.

Ivan's was as dark as the depths of a hooker's anus inside, but the main room was filled with neon silhouettes of cowboys and horses, giving the space a warm glow. The art actually was kind of beautiful. The place wasn't too big, but it was packed. With adult males. There were exactly zero other thirteen-year-old child-adults (like myself) there, so I was getting disapproving stares from pretty much everyone I looked at. I was still wearing my aubergine-hued tux, by the way, and on my upper lip was the teeniest little mustache of soft wispy pubic-like hairs.

"So, Joshy—" said the skeleton man.

"Please don't call me that."

"Your dad here says you want to become a man." And then he did something that resembled a laugh mixed with the cough of someone who is shortly going to die.

I looked at my dad, who was eyeing a passing topless woman carrying a platter of sushi and liquor. "I thought I already was a man?"

He was transfixed.

"Dad," I said louder.

"Yeah, yeah. He's here to become a man. Where's our table?"

Scary Thin pointed us in the direction of our table, and out of nowhere a guy who looked like a bouncer in all black appeared and ushered us toward the corner of the club. "Deuces Are Wild" by Aerosmith was playing, or some other sick fucking song. One of the tables we walked past was covered in napkins, and on top of the napkins were chicken wings, probably a hundred chicken wings, just laid out. This made me feel much more comfortable for some reason.

"Here you go, gentlemen," the big guy said as we sat at our table. "Ivan says hello, and Martinka should be over in just a few minutes."

As he said that last bit about Maria or whoever, he looked down at me and winked and then shot me with an imaginary gun made out of his fat fingers and then blew away the imaginary smoke. I think I LOL'd, to be honest. Then he was gone.

"Not bad!" my dad shouted over the music.

"Yeah, I guess. Who's Ivan?"

"I've known Ivan for forty years, He's a...good guy. Has a great tattoo of a panther."

My dad had never been "cool," meaning he wasn't particularly fun or into awesome stuff. To me, he was a frugal, responsible, sensible-shoe-wearing Russian radiologist who had worked hard literally all his life. I knew of his rough-Brooklyn-streets upbringing, but he never talked about it, long ago having left it for the far more upscale lifestyle. He wanted nothing to do with the

Russians he grew up with, the ones who don track suits and gold chains and commit tax fraud with no fear of prosecution (because American prison is essentially Club Med for them compared to the Eastern European jails, where rats would gnaw your penis off). My dad shied away from this upbringing and those people, but that night I got my first glimpse into his past. He knew a guy named Ivan with a tattoo of a panther? That was pretty cool. We were also at a strip club, which I was just starting to realize was very awesome.

"Have you been here before? Has Mom been here?"

I didn't press him about whether or not my mom had ever been to this shithole. But I would've felt way safer if I knew she had been. I was learning that a big part of being a man is feeling unsafe and being okay with that.

All of the spotlights in the place shot over to the main stage, and the room erupted with applause and cheers in Russian. Everyone in the club was Russian. The music stopped and a woman wearing chaps, cow-print stiletto heels, and a matching cowboy hat walked out. I could see her pussy. Now that I think about it, this may have been my first pussy. When was yours?

"Nice pussy!" I shouted over to my dad, who was now sipping on a beer. It just seemed like the appropriate thing for a straight guy to say. We were both shocked that I said it, and I was unsure how my dad would react. "Come on now, show some class," he said, and then he threw me a wink.

I noticed that a can of Coke with a straw in it had materialized on the table in front of me. *Okay, this isn't so weird*, I thought. I just needed to prove to my dad that I'm not gay with a few more comments like that, then it wouldn't be long before I could go home and eat cake with my mom.

I reached down to take a sip of my Coke, but before I could grab it, I felt two hands on my shoulders. Then the hands creeped down my chest, caressing the lapels of my suit and finally landing in my lap. Then I felt two large breasts cup either side of my face like a huge pair of foamy headphones. It was like fucking Teets by Dr. Dre!!!!! HAHAHAHAHAHA. OK, wait, no, so this is what happened next: My head was covered in boob, my hand was frozen mid-soda-reach, and I could feel that my tiny dick was starting to finally realize that he was in a strip club, because I had a semi.

"Wait—" I started to shout at my dad, but the woman who was connected to the tits spun my chair around (this chair is on wheels?), knelt down to my level, and I was face-to-face with her.

"Hello, darling," she said in a husky Russian accent. She had thick, curly black hair and a kind, handsome face. Her hands touched my thighs, and her hands were rough from years of working at factory in Mother Russia. (Just guessing. But probably.) She had a scar on her stomach, from a knife fight in the streets of the old country. (Again, just guessing. But it's the only thing that makes sense.)

"Hello," I said.

"My name Martinka."

"Okay."

"You want me to have you good sexy time, yes?"

"Um. Sex? Really?" I wondered if strip clubs were actually fuck clubs. At the time, there was one guy at my school who had actually fucked. His name was Mark. He was super tan and good at basketball and wore a hemp necklace. Having sex made him a legend. Was I about to join that sacred fraternity?

"You are sweet, sweet, little angel boy. So cute and chubby and delicious. I have son your age but not cute like you. Look at these eyes." She ruffled my hair and smiled so big. She was genuinely being such a sweet lady to me. I was completely hard at this point. I basically had a diamond stud in my pants. I was also still very much thirteen years old, which meant I could blow my load any minute. She stood up and put her hands on my shoulders, then sat down on my lap, straddling me. And my boner. I was glad that most everyone around me was watching the cowgirl pussy show on stage instead of the husky kid with a boner show at my table. I couldn't deal with any attention at the moment. It was awkward enough that my dad was sitting across the table from us.

She flopped her soft, real tits all over my face. *Is she gonna fuck me right here in front of my dad?* Then Martinka removed her tits from my head, turned around, put her hands on the ground, shook her ass in my face, and without warning kicked her legs up and over me, landed her heels on the table behind my chair, and put her vagina inches from my sweet angel face. I came in my pants. I mean that sincerely—a small circular stain of seed began increasing in size on my pant leg.

*"Dad?!"* I shouted to the universe. Looking back, that was probably a really creepy thing to say.

Martinka looked at me, upside down, through her arms. Then down at my suit pants. Dark blotches had formed around my dick area. She flipped her body around, her legs floated back to the ground with grace, and she stood back up dramatically because she was obviously a gymnast at age thirteen as well as a stripper, like all Russian women.

"He's not gay," she said to my dad, who came rushing over to look at me sitting frozen, horrified, in the chair.

"Oh, wow. Josh…"

After that, all I remember is my dad handing Martinka a stack of bills and then grabbing me by the arm and rushing me out of there as fast as he could. Before we walked out I told her to stop using a curling iron because it was frying her hair and sucking out all of its natural radiance and shine. My dad overheard me giving the stripper hair advice and it almost set off his gay-son alarm, but my spooging in my pants had pretty much made it clear to him that I was a young man who liked vaginas.

The car ride home was incredibly awkward. My dad blasted AM radio to drown out our mutual confusion and shame. We didn't speak once, except for in the final moment as we pulled up to our apartment. As I unbuckled my seat belt, my dad turned to me and said, "I'm proud of you. Tell your mother we ran out of gas."

I've spent the rest of my life trying to make my dad as proud of me as he was that night when I came in my pants at Ivan's Sexy Rodeo at midnight on the night of my bar mitzvah. No matter what I do, it'll never happen.

'm sure that most of the people reading this book are like me and don't really read that many books. It's pretty crazy, to me, that people still read books at all. It's so nineties to read. My brain has become so used to looking at Buzzfeed articles on the Internet like "The Top 10 Times Rihanna Was on a Beach" that having to read and process an entire book freaks me out. Many times I have my interns read to me. So when I was putting this whole thing together, I decided that I needed to add in a few moments throughout the book that could serve as little breaks for all of our brains. Like rest stops along the highway where you can refuel, get a thirty-two-ounce diet beverage, and check in with all of your social media accounts.

They will be a mix of some poetry I wrote while sitting on a fucking windowsill as raindrops pattered against the glass, some inspirational recipes that I use in my everyday life, and some excerpts from my childhood diary that are so disturbing it will become totally clear to you how I became the weirdo that I am today. Also, there will be some very chill coupons to clip out and use in your real life, because, well, *give the people what they want*. And I have also included a selection of coloring book pages based on dreams that I've had.

Reading is hard, and there are a lot of long chapters, but hopefully these little interludes will help you get through the book without getting frustrated and making you start to hate me.

## FAT JEW'S CARB-FREE SMOOTHIE THAT WILL MAKE YOU FEEL GOOD

I went to the doctor recently, and after performing my physical he alerted me that since I have recently turned thirty, it's time to start "taking care of myself," to start "respecting my body," and to "stop drinking gravy," all of which are things I have never excelled in. He alerted me that my intake of roughly six thousand calories a day in complex carbohydrates (eating like you're getting ready to run a marathon but then just sitting on your couch watching a *Cops* marathon) is apparently not a good long-term health plan, and I need to alter my diet. But in the interest of not dying before I get rich enough to become legendarily eccentric, get a boob job, and travel to space, I've decided to start making healthy smoothies (not awesome smoothies like the ones you get at a mall in Ohio that will give you diabetes immediately).

Juice and smoothie culture are obviously very LA, and I'm not going to sip a Swiss chard (it's a vegetable that I've heard of) with chia seeds concoction like I'm Tori fucking Spelling. I had to do this my way. A normal smoothie doesn't fill an extra large man like me up, so this had to be special. Dr. Rosenblattstein (seriously, my doctor has the Jewiest name in the history of Jews [and doctors]) told me to get protein by eating lots of meat, so I decided to base my smoothies around that. Since I'm such a giver and want you to be happy and healthy, I'm going to share my recipe with you. I'm like the thick-as-fuck Dr. Oz.

## Carb-Free Smoothie   Servings: 1

- A large bags of beef jerky (preferably Jack Links, could be Oberto if you're poor)
- 1/2 tablespoon A1 sauce
- 5 teaspoons sriracha
- 10 Xanax pills (optional but also kinda not optional)
- 7 ice cubes

Combine all items in a blender. Blend until smooth. Sit on couch and watch "The Real Housewives of Atlanta." cheer when someone's weave gets ripped out. then fall asleep not-at-all hungry.

### Nutrition: (per serving)
750 cals. 4 g fat. 0.8 g sat fat. 2,950 mg sodium. 0 grams of motherfucking carbs. 1.5 g fiber. 96 g protein

# A HAIKU 4 U:

Goldie Hawn: still hot

I would really eat her butt

after spinning class

## WILL SMITH: A POEM

Just spending another day

wondering why they changed the mom on Fresh Prince of

Bel-Air from the dark one to a much lighter one

and didn't say shit about it

Right?

There's a kid in my class named chris
and he's cool. We hang out sometimes
at my friend Doug's house. Doug's
house is the best because he
has a Nintendo power glove
and always has fruit roll-ups
and his dad is divorced from his
mom and they are rich. Me and
Chris were at Doug's house for
a sleepover and chris was changing
into his sleep clothes and i saw his
peenuss and it was really big.
I have a peenuss too but it looks

# JOSHUA

different and Much More little.
chris's peenuss was really big
and cool i wish i had one like
that. Also when we play
basketball chris is the best
player he makes all his shots.
Michael Jordan is the best basketball
player ever and i bet he has a big
peenuss to because he is black
and i saw another black man
at my tennis center and he was
showering and his penuss was big
and black. I want a big peenuss and to
be good at basketball and very tall. How do you get black

THIS COUPON IS GOOD FOR:

THIS COUPON IS GOOD FOR:

An entire day of

STFU

# HOW TO HANG A SHELF

1. Buy the shelf you want to hang.

2. Compile the tools necessary.

3. Lay out all materials.

4. Begin to feel massive anxiety.

5. Feel your body temperature rising quickly.

6. Lay on the floor in fetal position, crying.

7. Lash out at whoever is in the closest physical proximity to you for absolutely no reason.

8. Continue weeping.

7. Crawl to your computer and use craigslist to hire a handy man with rough hands who actually knows how to do stuff besides looking at social media to come over and hang your shelf for way too much money.

THIS COUPON IS GOOD FOR:

ONE VENTI
SOY CARAMEL
HALF CAF
ICED LATTE
(3 PUMPS)

# THIS COUPON IS GOOD FOR:

## ONE NIGHT OF DESIGNATED DRIVING

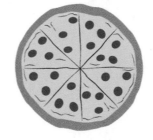

# THE SEVEN WONDERS OF MY DICK

osh, are you packed?" my mom screamed from her room.

Fourteen-year-old me was in the bathroom, shitting and playing *Kung Fu Master* on my Gameboy. I'd forgotten we were going on a family trip to England and we were leaving the next day, so, no, not packed at all.

"Yeah, I'm packed!" I shouted.

"Are you really, or is that a lie and I need to come do it for you?"

"Mom, I'm packed. I promise!"

"Okay, but you only say you promise when you're lying."

"Can I please *take a shit in peace?*"

"Don't say that word to me. It's so ugly when you shout it."

"*Fuck!*" I died. Game over, the end.

"Josh!!" she yelled, her voice getting closer.

"Sorry. My game."

"What?!"

"Never mind! I'll pack after I'm done in here."

"Josh!"

"I. Will. Pack. I need to *poopy*," I said in a slurred, mentally handicapped person's voice (my editor told me that the word *retarded* is offensive), which was very funny to me at that point in my life and still is a little funny. I have nothing to hide here.

"You need to pack as soon as you come out of the bathroom." I could almost hear her hot and heavy breath on the door. She was always *very* stressed about traveling. Going on a trip basically turned my mom into Bane from *The Dark Knight Rises*...

"Fine," I offered under my breath while wiping my ass. I should mention that I'd moved out of my gay bar mitzvah phase and into my pot/rap music phase. I couldn't grasp why she'd never let me wear one outfit for an entire week when I was traveling, like I wanted to. It worked fine for me at summer camp, but she'd never understand that. My mom's not about that life.

"Thank you," she said sweetly and walked away from the bathroom door.

I pulled out the suitcase from under my bed, threw in a bunch of crumpled hoodies and boxers, and then refocused my energy on *Kung Fu Master*.

My parents are those kind of very annoying people who are obsessed with "seeing" the world, so when I was a teenager they took my brother and me on some crazy trips, like ones where people ask why you would bring children to that. I saw tons of shit that most people only ever see in pictures. Paris, Rome, Beijing, Moscow, Prague, Auckland, Georgia (the country), the Ukraine,

Laos. Maybe this sounds awesome to you, but as a spoiled piece of shit kid, I hated this about them. I felt like I was constantly on another plane to somewhere lame, while, to be quite fucking honest, all I wanted to do was stay in New York and steal weed from my friends so I could smoke it with my other friends. I really didn't want to see a ruined temple with my dad. It meant nothing to me. My parents are like scenic memory hoarders or something. They were constantly trying to make me a better person with worldly perspective, and it was wildly annoying.

I guess as an adult (okay, man-child) I could take the view that my parents were genuinely interested in experiencing the wonders of our magical planet and that they just wanted to share those amazing adventures with me. But I choose not to. I feel that maintaining some aspects of my teen angst keeps me fresh and connected to all my teen fans with shitty attitudes.

So the next morning we were off to the United Kingdom. England was whatever, double-decker buses, red telephone booths, crumpets, hegemony, I get it. It's fine. But for the *highlight* of our England trip, my parents took my brother and me to Stonehenge to see this crazy laser show (which was a thing they did there in the early nineties). The woman who seated us handed us each a blanket and a lawn chair. I set up my chair about ten feet behind my parents and my brother, as an act of peaceful rebellion from my family.

"You good?" my dad asked me, looking back.

"Yeah. When is this supposed to start?" I asked, genuinely excited.

"Any minute," replied my mom, also without turning around. "Do you need another blanket?" she asked. My mom and dad were having a blast on this fucking England trip. My dad walked around in this dumb plaid hat he got at the hotel shop, and my mom kept taking pictures with the new camera that my dad had gotten her for their anniversary. They were holding hands and acting like teenagers. Both of them had never been to Stonehenge, and you could tell they were just loving the whole *look how fucking old the place is* thing.

Before I could respond, the show started. Green, blue, and pink lasers shot out from all corners of the rock formation. Some dramatic classical music played. The lasers became increasingly frantic as the song crescendoed. A few minutes into the show I realized that I had my hand on my dick, under the blanket. I mean I was fucking preteen. I got hard once when my Spanish tutor said a word that sounded like "fuentes." I got hard all the time for no reason at all. Not to mention that I was basically touching my dick at all times. It's a thing. Ask anyone who is male and was, at some point in his life, a fourteen-year-old.

I was definitely getting aroused by the show *and* the fact that I was in such a public place was kind of playing into, too. So I was like OK...*fuck this. I'm already halfway down this road...the journey has begun...it is my destiny to jerk off under this blanket here.*

About forty seconds later, I was done.

The result was minimal enough that there was no real trace

of my excellent and exhilarating decision to masturbate under a fleece blanket not ten feet from my parents at *fucking Stonehenge!*

It was amazing. *The best* jack-off session that I'd ever experienced in my life.

I felt cool. I *was* cool. I was overcome by a sense of accomplishment. When you're fourteen, pulling off this type of stunt successfully means something.

"Well, was that amazing or what?!" my mom said as the show finished, looking back at me in my lawn chair.

"Yeah, Mom, that was really cool," I responded as I carefully folded my blanket. "Definitely the best part of the trip so far."

My gears were turning. Stonehenge would become the first stop on a very specific journey in my life. When we returned home to New York, I felt like I was something was different. Like, my eyes had been opened to a whole new way of seeing and thinking about the world. I'd been exposed to a higher level of sexual existence, and I was not about to let go of it. I was breaking down barriers and exploring uncharted territory. I was essentially the Magellan of masturbation. But I didn't really know how to go about existing on this level because I was *fourteen.* So I kinda just kept my Stonehenge moment on the back burner.

It wasn't until the next year, when our parents took us to Paris, that my mind began to awaken to all the possibilities. I was sitting with my brother in coach, while my parents sat in first class. That was the way they did things. Because they said they could afford it, and one day we'd be able to do that if we *focused on our school work.* As fifteen-year-old me sat there on the plane thinking about how much he didn't give a shit about croissants and berets, I noticed the *Departures* magazine that was in the seat back pocket in front of me. It had a big picture of the Eiffel Tower on it. My eyes lit up. I had a major breakthrough/realization. I was *alive!*

"You definitely think we're gonna go to the Eiffel Tower?" I turned and excitedly asked my brother, Avi. (Side note: This is not his real name, but I promised I would change it to protect his identity. Unfortunately for him, a simple Google search will reveal his name.)

"Errr...what?"

I didn't realize it but he was already asleep.

"Yeah," he said groggily, annoyed.

"Anyway, what I was saying was, you think we're gonna go to the Eiffel Tower or no?"

"Why do you care? You don't even wanna go on this trip."

"Yeah, I do."

"Did you not tell Mom last night that you were coming down with leg cancer and you thought it'd be best if you stayed home?"

I had 100 percent said that exact thing to my parents the night before over Chinese food. They barely reacted.

"Yeah, whatever, I woke up feeling much better today," I said. "But for real, let's make sure we go to the Eiffel Tower, okay? Yeah?!"

Avi winced. I was basically shouting, overwhelmed by the spirit in me, a new purpose in life. I was going to be the first man ever, in the history of all men, to masturbate at every important/ renowned/wondrous tourist destination across planet Earth. *Me!*

It was gonna be *me*!!! I needed to figure out if this was the kind of thing that you could get into the *Guinness Book of World Records* for. Probably not, but I wanted to double-check.

Obviously my parents were planning a visit to the tower, because how fucking dumb would it be to go to Paris and not see the Eiffel Tower? We went the very next day, and I was able to immediately locate a porta-potty to jerk off in. You could see the sky-scraping wrought iron tower through the slitted window vent at the top of the potty. I stared intensely at it as I stroked. Another success. It smelled like a fucking diaper in there, but I actually jerked off twice because you can do that type of thing when you're fifteen.

Now it was official. I was a man with a plan (and a three-inch penis): epic global masturbation. This, if accomplished, would make me new friends every time I told the story, for the rest of my life. From that trip on I started to take a real interest in where my parents took us next. They were happy I cared, so they pretty much let me pick the next few destinations. Rather, they were letting my dick pick.

I honestly need to pat myself on the back here. I was doing some very killer work at such a young age. Think about what we're talking about here. *I was jerking off at the wonders of the world!* Looking back, it actually seems crazy that I did this. I had a beautiful mind. It's not that hard to see how I ended up being the *adult me* when you look at the kind of shit I was into as an adolescent.

I managed to continue my spree of utter awesomeness the following year at the Egyptian pyramids (behind a helicopter on a landing pad—I'm dead serious), the Leaning Tower of Pisa the following year (alone, at night, on the lawn, baggy sweatpants), but then came my biggest challenge. My Iron Man, my holy grail, my Moby Dick: the Great Wall of China. This would be, by far, the hardest location on the planet Earth to pull off my stunt. But I was locked in, and nothing was going to stand in my way.

If you've never been to the Great Wall, you're not missing much. It's actually horrendous. It's a sea of people who are basically just standing *on* the thing that they came to see, thus making it impossible to actually see anything. For my purposes, the wall was very much exposed, and there's nothing around it. It's the Everest of wonder tugs. It was clear from the moment that we pulled up that I was going to have to lose my family on purpose to even scout out possible jerking locations. Hungry and focused, I ditched my family, and for about an hour I scoured every nook and cranny of the area. It was *sooooooo* crowded. I weaved in and out of the multiracial mob of human beings and ended up in front of this tiny staircase that led up to this little tower that overlooked a good stretch of the wall. *Shhhwing!*

But the whole vibe in China is *not chill*, so my normal sexual excitement about these types of moments was not as high as usual.

I thought about Lil' Kim's tits (it was the nineties, so obviously) and then looked out onto to the wall to do the deed. It was a cold day, which didn't help things either.

*"You not allowed go here!"* shouted an aggressive Chinese voice from behind me, literally at the moment I started cumming. I pushed my dick against my leg and shot a lumpy spray of semen downward.

The tower had provided me complete and total cover, so I thought I was in the clear. This dude must have followed me up there. *Fuck!!!!* My pants were very clearly unbuckled, and he could probably see that from where he was standing.

"Ahhhhhhhh!!! No!!!! What?!!!!!" I shouted back to him without turning around, obviously. I was fully prepared to be shot in the back. I just hoped he would make it quick. As slowly and as quietly as humanly possible, I began zipping my fly and putting my belt through the buckle.

"No, no, you. *You* need go out from *here!*" the man yelled. I turned around and looked at him. He was a small Chinese man in some sort of beige uniform and little hat. There was a gun on his belt. Or a flashlight, I don't know. It totally could've been a gun.

"Okay, Okay, Okay! I got lost!" I shouted back at him, scrambling to get my shit together enough to reenter the world. I normally took five minutes after each session to relax and reflect. China had offered me no such moment.

I was visibly shaken when I found my parents, who had clearly been frightened by my disappearance.

"Where the hell were you?" my dad demanded.

"I got lost. Let's just go," I said, trying to catch my breath.

"We almost called the embassy, Josh," added my mom, on the verge of tears. "You need to be more careful. This isn't New York City. They don't understand you here. They'll take you away and we'll never see you again. *You do not want to end up in a Chinese prison!*"

"Relax, Mom. This isn't North Korea," Avi said.

"Yeah, exactly. Calm down. I just had to pee and couldn't find a good spot," I explained.

"Did you pee on the wall?!" asked my Mom, horrified.

"No, no. It's fine. The bathroom had a long line and then I walked all the way to this other one that ended up being out of service...it doesn't matter," I said. "I just really need to get out of here. This place is so crazy."

So many questions rushed through my head as we drove down the windy road and away from the Wall. *Had that guy seen me mid-jerk-off? Are there cameras at the Great Wall of China? Did the Chinese government now know my face and what my penis looks like, and would they let me leave the country or would I be interrogated (and tortured?) at the airport?*

My leg was doused with jizz and I was shaken up, but I knew I had done it, and I was brimming with pride. I'd been on this epic adventure for five years. It was now a large piece of who I was as a human being. It was probably the main thing about me, actually. The Wall felt like it was my own personal Vietnam. It had made me doubt everything I believed in, but I fought through it and I was safe now.

Unfortunately, that was the last time I'd have the pleasure of pleasuring myself in eyeshot of true manmade beauty. I wanted the Taj Mahal so bad, but my parents went when I had a serious girlfriend who looked like Jon Lovitz and who I wanted to stay home and fingerblast for days on end. Also, the China situation had really upset me, and I wasn't sure I was ready to start spilling seed internationally again. Who knows? Maybe one day I'll make it to the Taj Mahal. It's important to have dreams and to hold on to them tightly. *May all your dreams cummmmmm true!!!!*

6.iii

127 MINUTES

et me start off by saying that I love drugs. Love them. Love-love-*love* them. Kids, stay in drugs, don't do school.

Now that we've established my undying love for substances, let me explain. Drugs, which have ruined the lives of so many, can be awesome if you know how to use them. You just have to be reasonable and not be a human with an addictive personality, and then they're sooooo fun. I've basically tried every drug (I'm sure there is some shit in the Ukraine that makes your face physically melt off that I haven't gotten hold of), and at a certain point I was doing new ones just so I could say I had done them all.

I really had no desire to do heroin, but at that point it was the only thing left on my list and just had to be done. It's no different than when you were a kid and there was a set of toys that said "Collect all 10!" and you had to have all ten. Also, heroin sucks. I barfed all over my own bare feet and then sat and watched *The Price Is Right* for a bunch of hours, it was not fun. But I have done it all: uppers, downers, barbies, benzos, tutti-frutti, trail mix, liquid lady, that John McCain (yes, coke), dust, foxy, 2CB, DMT, crystal, ecstasy, Thorazine, rophenol, quaaludes, special K, opium, ayahuasca, peyote...the list goes on and on. I always knew that one day, when I wrote a book, I could say I had done them all.

*Today is that day, and it was so worth it.*

But for all that experimentation, all the different types of substances I've abused my body with, my first love has always been magic mushrooms. I would recommend shrooms to anyone, whether a hardcore drug user or someone who only smokes pot on an occasional Sunday and watches twelve straight hours of Netflix. Shrooms are fun, they grow in the earth (if that kind of thing makes you feel better), and they are a hallucinogen, but they're nothing like LSD. When you take acid, you never know what might happen. You might think all your fingers have turned into tiny penises and that your friend is a literal dragon with a gimp mask on who wants to kill you. You actually see stuff. But on shrooms, you basically feel strange, think the floor is moving a little bit, but *everything is fun*. No, really, you could be in a library eating a muffin for an entire day and your takeaway of the experience would be that you had an incredible time.

One spring weekend when I was in college, some friends and I took a camping trip to a state park about an hour outside Manhattan, and the entire goal was to eat shrooms and be weird. We had done these types of excursions before, and most of the time they ended up with somebody getting naked and falling asleep in some shrubs. For those of you who don't know, Jews are *not* outdoorsy. Now I'm sure you can find a Jew in Colorado with dreads who is a whitewater rafting instructor and knows how to kill a water buffalo and sleep inside its carcass to keep warm, but he is basically the only one. Jews are indoor creatures—even their natural outdoor habitats are indoors: screened-in porches and huge umbrellas at the beach. We don't camp, and despite persevering within society amid thousands of years of religious persecution, we are actually very poor survivalists.

If I had to start a fire in order to survive in the wilderness, I would probably just curl up into the fetal position, weep myself to sleep in a pile of leaves, and hope I got mauled by a wild boar. We don't hunt food, we order it. But there we were, four Jews who all grew up in New York City thinking that a state park (which had a gift shop, LOL) was the wilderness.

It was me, Adam, Adam, and Brett. Yes, two guys named Adam. One was Silverman (Jewy name) and the other was Goldberg-Lipschultz (Jewier name). We drove Jewiest Adam's mom's Subaru (she's a lesbian who came out when we were in high school, so of course she had to get a Subaru; it's sort of the official car of the New York lesbian mom). The shrooms were bought from a guy named Laser Man, a neighborhood weirdo who must have been in his fifties. He was a beatnik holdover from the much more bohemian New York City of yesteryear. Dude was a *legit maniac*. I was once saw him eating a raw potato like an apple, just biting right into it. Laser Man was a guy who could "get things," and one of those things was definitely magic mushrooms. I think actually maybe that's all he could get. We bought enough for ten people, piled in the lesbomobile, cranked some Ashanti (it was hot at the time, so get over it; I'm not trying to please you), and headed into the great outdoors.

We arrived in the late afternoon and immediately started setting up camp. It was one of those parks with mostly families in RVs on some sort of continental United States road trip, and we were definitely going to scar some of their children. Brett is half-Jewish and had been to some sort of Outward Bound survival program thing, so he knew how to pitch a tent (I'm honestly not even sure that's what you call making a tent). Once we were all set up, it was time to get wild. We ate the shrooms, cracked a few shitty domestic beers, and got ready to make some memories.

"I don't feel anything," Brett said after like thirty minutes.

"Just wait," I said. "We're not gonna be those guys who don't feel anything so they eat more and then freak out because they ate too much."

We waited a couple more minutes, then decided to become exactly those guys.

After eating twice the recommended dosage, we decided to go on a walk. It was on that first foray into the wilderness that

everyone realized that we were fully in outer space. We were immediately ravenous and dehydrated. The provisions we'd brought with us were comical: one small bottle of Poland Spring water, forty packs of cigarettes, a small bag of marijuana, one Clif energy bar that was in the glove compartment of the lesbian's Subaru, and a machete. Yes, one of those objects seems way more helpful than the others. We walked around aimlessly for a while, smoking cigarettes and talking about how nobody would ever be funnier than Adam Sandler (update: we were wrong), and eventually we came upon a stream. Maybe it was a creek? Is there a fucking difference? In retrospect, this stream was shitty and small, but being that we were deep in the throes of a shroom journey, it looked to me like we were basically in Nicaragua under a waterfall surrounded by exotic animals.

The Adams, Brett, and I decided to get shirtless and trudge through the stream (shoes stayed on, but it seemed necessary at the time to only remove our shirts). It felt like we walked about one hundred miles, but it was probably closer to one hundred yards.

One of the Adams stopped.

"Guys, I have a question. Are you ready for this?"

I stared at him in awe, like he was fucking Plato, about to say something so deep and philosophical that it would shatter my brain into a million tiny pieces.

"Does the alphabet have to be in the order that it's in? It would still work if it wasn't, right?"

"Oh my God," Brett whispered. "He's fucking right."

We all stood there motionless, staring at Adam like he had just discovered science. He actually *had* shattered my brain into a million tiny pieces. His question was so deep that it *still* shatters my brain.

Then Adam 2 broke out singing the ABCs, but in a different order:

"B, K, R, S, T, H, Y, C, F, M, L, O, E, D, X, N, I, P, J, Q, A, G, W, U, V, Z."

"Now I know my BKRs," I sang.

*"We are high on fucking drugs,"* Adam 1 belted out triumphantly.

We were totally fucked up.

The stream came to an end and the landscape opened upon a large forested area. What came next resembled a pack of teenaged Larry Davids reenacting *The Lord of the Flies*. We proceeded to paint our faces with green nose zinc that Adam 1 brought to keep his nose safe from the sun, which is hilarious because he thought it was OK to take hallucinogenic drugs and wander around a forest, but God forbid he get sunburned on his nose. So now our faces are painted green and we're running around in our underpants thinking we're in fucking Vietnam, having the time of our lives.

At one point Brett jumped out of a tree and tackled me, we're both in our underpants (he was wearing dad-style white briefs), and it was very *Brokeback Mountain* in the best possible way. Adam 2 found a tiny lizard, and we were all were completely entranced by it.

"I think we've discovered a new species!" he screamed, and we all came running over.

"Whoa," I said, "this is like...life."

LOL. No, seriously, what a bunch of college morons.

We thought we'd discovered a new breed of animal that needed to be written about by scientists, when in fact we'd literally found the most basic lizard that can be found anywhere. After walking around for a few more hours, smoking a joint, and discussing how Jamie Lee Curtis used to be a hermaphrodite and had a dick (which is true), we were dirty and sweaty and tripping and happy.

Heading back to camp, we began walking along the stream from earlier. I was tripping balls and wearing Birkenstocks with socks, so I obviously fell behind the group. I could hear the guys ahead of me so I wasn't worried, until I dropped the unlit cigarette I was holding and decided to get on all fours and look for it. *Why would I do that?* We had roughly four thousand cigarettes with us; finding this one was completely unnecessary. After frantically searching for a minute or two, like I had lost a check for a billion dollars, I finally found it. I was overjoyed. A warm tear may have even rolled down my cheek. It was a glorious moment.

It was only when I stood up and moved on from my personal triumph that I realized my boys were long gone. I was also at my highest level of shrooming. I had also eaten some tree bark earlier just to be funny (it wasn't that funny) and was pretty sure I was going to shit my pants.

Smashcut to an hour later. I'd been wandering and thinking I'd be killed by natives (we're an hour outside of New York City). This is when I was severely lost. Like Lost. Yes, like the popular television show. I might as well have been on that island, that's how stranded I felt. In the distance I also heard what I thought was a wolf but may have been a howling frat boy on a camping excursion from the nearby college.

Then I realized what to do. I drew a line connecting the sun down to the horizon. In northern latitudes this will give an approximation of cardinal south. It works best when the sun is high in the sky, but this would have to do...AHAHAHAHHAHAHA just kidding. I don't know shit about that stuff. So I just sat on the ground and smoked cigarettes for a while until I fell asleep in a pile of leaves.

When I woke up I wasn't sure if ten minutes had passed or ten days. The shrooms were still melting my mind and I was exhausted. The sun. It was hot. So hot. What I was going to do? How was I going to survive? The guys probably assumed I had gone on a personal solo mission to do crazy stuff. I figured that once the shrooms wore off and I didn't come back, they'd get worried. I waited for what felt like hours, but was probably closer to twenty minutes.

I decided then that despite all my Jewish instincts, I was going to conquer the wilderness and survive. I would make all my Jewish forefathers who hate the outdoors proud, like Woody

Allen and my uncle Murray. I rummaged through my pockets and besides some loose marijuana, the only thing I had was a pen. I found a napkin in the bushes from a Ruby Tuesday restaurant and started journaling.

**HOUR 1:** If I happened to die, I wanted a record of my last moments.

**HOUR 3:** Starving, haven't eaten in a couple hours. I think I'm dying. Picked a berry but am too afraid to eat it. Licked it once to get some flavor. Nope.

**HOUR 4:** Why won't these shrooms wear off????????

**HOUR 5:** Walked around more, screaming my friends' names. They are all way too high to care enough about where I am, or even realize that I'm gone, for that matter. I'm definitely on my own at this point. Thought I heard an animal in the bushes and approached it thinking I could kill it and eat it. It was actually a man, I think he was a mountain man, taking a shit. He screamed something horrible at me. When I came back to seek assistance from him, he was gone. His fecal matter smelled horrendous; he is definitely sick. I wonder if he is stranded, too, and had to just live out here and make a life like Tom Hanks in *Castaway* and be best friends with a piece of sporting equipment.

**HOUR 6:** Saw a deer. If I could somehow kill it, I could skin it and sleep inside of its carcass. LOL.

**Hour 100 it feels like:** As I lay here, dying, I think about all the things I want to say to people that I was never able to say. What can I say that nobody ever knew, my deepest secret…oh wait, I've got it. I've never seen *Titanic* and have lied my whole life about it. Also, I once let a guy give me a blowjob for ten seconds at a party.

**Hour 8 (????):** Ate the berry. Immediately made myself vomit.

**Nighttime:** It's getting dark so I needed to make a fire. Rubbed some sticks together—is this a thing that can actually happen? No way. Seriously, have you ever tried that?

**More Nighttime:** I think I'm dead. Is this what being dead feels like. Am I a ghost? I'm going to watch so many people masturbating if I am.

I wasn't dead because I woke up at daybreak in a pile of leaves and my own piss. I was alive. Now dead sober, I had to find the others. Were they OK? This was my moment. I had to have strength to get out of this situation. I wanted to live. I needed to live. A calm came over me, and I knew I'd be able to fight through whatever the next few hours, days, or even weeks had in store for me. I have always been a fighter and I wasn't going to give up now. Using all my remaining strength, I lifted myself off the ground and began walking through the woods. The sun was peeking out from behind some trees, and I knew that soon enough it would beat mercilessly upon me. I had to find water if I was going to survive.

Now that I was not high I realized that the woods were not as intense as they were before. In fact, it was more like shrubbery.

Two minutes later (no, seriously, two minutes) the woods (we'll still call them that) opened up on a parking lot. I was standing in the fucking parking lot of a CVS. This whole time I'd thought I was stranded in the wilderness, with no water, no food, no end in sight. I was literally one thousand yards from a tremendous amount of Diet Coke.

# 7.

# TAMPA BAY PREGNANT WOMEN'S BIKINI CONTEST

A few years ago, a local radio station in Tampa Bay, Florida, which I believe was called 104.2 The Jungle, contacted me through Twitter to ask if I'd be the judge at a "hot bikini body" contest for pregnant women. (Seriously, this exists.) When the radio producer, Bryyan (and I swear that's how he spelled it. *Two fucking Ys???*), initially got in touch, I was ecstatic. Pregnant women in thongs vying for a $750 cash prize and a gift certificate to a local steak house, and I get to pick the winner? *Sign me the fuck up.* I wondered why I hadn't invented it. And so, Bryyan signed me up. Full disclosure: When I was twelve I had this hot babysitter named Shannon, who got teen pregnant (she was like eighteen), and I became obsessed with the idea that there was a baby inside her vagina. She was single and was bizarrely flirty with me. I always wanted to fuck her. This was my chance to live out that dream.

The night before the competition I flew into Tampa and checked into the motel Bryyan had arranged, then things took a very dark turn. The whole gig went from scummy and fun to scummy and terrifying. The motel was definitely haunted and located next to an abandoned old house with a sign that read PALMDALE HOME FOR BOYS, which honestly looked like it hadn't been open for a hundred years. In fear of being raped by the ghosts of a thousand molested orphans, I decided to find the closest place to get a drink, which ended up being a bar a few blocks away.

It was a sweaty walk, because Tampa is moist as fuck and the worst possible place. It's where you are likely to be murdered by a guy with a toe ring. Fortunately the Tampanese (not sure what you call people from Tampa. Tampanites? Tampons?) love air-conditioning, so when I walked into the bar, I was blasted with a polar vortex that soothed my overheated soul.

Now, I dig a wacky-ass bar scene as much as the next guy, but this place was mental. It looked like it was a filming location from an episode of *True Blood*. The bartender was in a tuxedo without the shirt (why?) and the sole patron, a guy in a Bart Simpson tank top who had a very *very* poorly made glass eye, was drinking a mojito.

So that particular Wednesday, while you were probably getting home from work, I was in Tampa Bay, Florida, drinking with a man who'd lost his eye "in a fight with a giant" (his words) and talking about what it feels like to have sex with pregnant women.

Needless to say, I got pretty hammered and woke up the

following day, back in my motel room. I grabbed a French Toast Slam breakfast at a Denny's and headed to the venue, which was some weird, old, truly horrible community center on the outskirts of town. The crowd was about a hundred guys, and it was absolutely the worst sampling of humanity imaginable. Take a second to step back and imagine the type of person who, first of all, is *available* to watch a contest at three p.m. on a Thursday, and, second, *wants* to see bikini-clad women who are very much with child dump water on themselves as they gyrate slowly on stage. There's an actual 100 percent chance that each one of those men was a fucking maniac.

The gig itself was pretty straightforward. It was a parade of preggo 4½'s, and then a few ridiculously hot, fuckable pregnant women. There were so many bad tattoos it was like heaven for me. I'm obsessed with people making horrible mistakes that are totally avoidable and completely unchangeable. The best was a tattoo of a "rose" on this chick's calf that had the word *baby* written under it in cursive.

The girl I crowned the "winner" was one of the really hot ones, but she wasn't the hottest. Her name was Kensy and she was sexy, but she wasn't my favorite. Also, did I mention her name was *Kensy*? I figured that the girl I chose as the winner would probably never fuck me, because she'd already gotten my approval. But the girl I gave the runner-up prize to would definitely be down. That's why I gave second place to this blonde named Nikki (people, hear me: naming your daughter Nikki almost guarantees that they'll end up in this type of situation), who had nice teeth and thick calves.

After the contest was officially over, I approached Nikki, congratulated her, and asked if she wanted to celebrate her runner-up status by letting me take her out for an ice cream sundae. She seemed genuinely excited by my offer.

"Really? With me?"

"Yeah, you were awesome up there. Let's go celebrate."

"Okay. That's so sweet of you. I'm Nikki, by the way."

"I know."

When we got to Baskin-Robbins, it became clear that Nikki was genuinely a really nice person.

"So I went to the University of Florida to become a marine biologist, because I love sharks. Like, I'm obsessed with sharks and stuff."

"Me, too," I lied. I fucking hate sharks. "Shark Week is my favorite week of the year, dude."

"That's so funny, I love Shark Week, too. So I was like studying really hard and stuff but then I met this shithead named Brendan who wore cargo shorts every day and quoted *Anchorman*. Something about him kept me coming back for more, and then in my junior year Brendan knocked me up and then pretty much disappeared. Which is kinda why I entered the contest. I really needed the money."

"Totally get it. Brendan sounds like he fucking sucks."

Nikki was relatively smart, her breath smelled like a basket of peaches, and she also told me in the course of our conversation that she couldn't eat around retarded people. Just like me!!!! We ended up sitting in that Baskin-Robbins for more than an hour and discussed things like how it was weird that both know the theme song to *The Fresh Prince of Bel-Air* but don't know the words to the national anthem. I convinced myself that Nikki was my soul mate. I was even a fan of her plan to name her son Detox, which, looking back, was possibly the worst idea of all time.

In case you don't already know it, pregnant women go through a phase where they get extremely horny. Given her body language and her constantly grabbing my leg when she laughed, Nikki was clearly looking to get banged, and she was not being shy about it. So when she invited me over to her condo, I knew it was on.

Her place was very Florida: lots of wall-to-wall carpeting and a framed poster on the wall that said "When the weather in life gets bad, dance in the rain." Based on her CD rack (having a CD rack nowadays is so, so dark) she clearly loved DMX as much as me, which was obviously a major turn-on. I moved things onto the couch, and we started mouth kissing. It was a little awkward at first on account of the fact that her belly was pretty fucking huge and in the way. I'm clearly not a small man, so I was very freaked out about crushing the baby. I was trying to be super careful while also trying to keep it sexy. Nikki was definitely sexually aggressive, and I was into that, but I was distracted by the other human being between us.

Then...I felt baby Detox kick me in the arm, which immediately made my penis sad and soft. I was confused by my emotions at that moment, so I excused myself to the bathroom as nonchalantly as I could. Staring into the mirror, I asked myself what the fuck was really going on here.

This whole trip I'd been dreaming about having sex with a pregnant woman. And now here it was, for the taking, and I was getting rattled. Was the kick a *sign?* That baby was defending his territory. "*Get the fuck out of here!*" he was saying. "Space occupied." But, you know what? *Screw Detox,* I thought. This was my time. Time to man up and be one with Nikki.

Like a returning hero, with my boner back on track, I stormed back into the living room, only to find her sleeping on the couch, peacefully, using my hoodie as a blanket. I'd been gone all of five minutes and here she was, sound asleep, like a little pregnant angel who enters bikini contests to win some extra money.

Standing there looking at Nikki, I suddenly realized that part of the reason I wanted to bang her was so I'd have a great story to tell my friends when I got back. I felt compelled to do something I never do: the right thing. So, I grabbed a blanket off of her bed and gently covered her with it. Then I left her $501 cash on her kitchen table (which, added to the $250 she won for being the runner-up, made a total of $751) with a note that said, "You're the real winner, Nikki." Then I left her place and went straight to the airport to try to get on an earlier flight, because there was no way in hell I was spending another night in that motel, which was undoubtedly covered in the semen of men even more horrible than myself.

Six months later, my Filipino intern Choo-choo called me to tell me I had gotten a Facebook message (yes, I have an intern who checks my Facebook messages) from a girl named Nikki telling

me that she'd decided against naming her son Detox and instead
had named him after me. I was truly touched and honored and
felt warm inside. To commemorate the moment, I did what felt
natural: I masturbated in the mirror, my breath fogging up the
surface, and whispered "you complete me" to myself.

# A CHRISTMAS
# MIRACLE

t was snowing on the night of the twenty-fourth and had been snowing for almost a week. New York City was basically frozen over, and due to a series of falling-outs I'd had over the past month, I was alone as fuck on Christmas Eve. I didn't have a girlfriend at the time, so I didn't have a girlfriend's family to spend it with. I guess there were a couple of Upper West Side goyim I could've tried to do something with, but as a Jew, I honestly don't give a fuck about Christmas activities. So I went in a different direction altogether and smoked marijuana alone in my West Village one bedroom and watched *Top Chef* with the sound off.

At around 11:30 p.m. I smelled non-weed smoke. It was thick, too, and coming through my front door and shit, like a movie. I was like...*wait? Am I high or dead or on fire?* An alarm went off and pulled me out of my stupor. I shot up and opened the front door and realized the alarm was coming from the smoke detector in my hallway. It was going off on every floor. We were all gonna die maybe? I walked back into my place, grabbed the one thing I wanted to save in that moment—my phone (and my cigarettes)—and started heading down the stairs from my third story walkup. I intentionally left my computer, thinking I might be able to get a new one from insurance if it got burned up, which is stupid because I'm pretty sure I didn't have homeowner's insurance. It was also strange how calm I was. Like the weed had put me in a very chill place. I was as bizarrely calm as Liam Neeson is whenever his daughter or someone he cares about is being kidnapped by Albanian sex traffickers.

"Josh! Okay. Am I glad to see you!" *What does that even mean*, I thought.

"Are you okay?" she continued. It was the yoga lady with bad teeth and big boobs from apartment 3A.

"I'm fine, dude."

"Okay! Good!" She wiped her forehead exaggeratingly. "I think we need to get out of here now, honey!"

"Yeah," I said and followed her down the hallway to the stairs.

On the way down to the street I ran into the rest of the people in my building who were home on Christmas Eve and were now being displaced by the fire. I still didn't know where it was coming from. No one did. But it was extremely smoky everywhere and it smelled all ashy and sick in the stairwell. There was the stoned, fat AIDS guy from 2C and the fashion PR woman with a pill problem from 4F, who was carrying some kind of small dog or ferret. Then came the two beautiful lesbians who lived in 2A, who I think were models (or actually, now that I think about it, they might be sisters and not lesbians). All of the occupants of the building were filing out like an odd class of adult children on a field trip. Everyone looked really scared and concerned for one another.

New York City is really strange in that way. You don't really know your neighbors in any intimate way. You basically live together, but you've never formally met. It's disgusting and magical and terrifying all at the same time.

It was freezing outside, but I was still pretty high from weed and very much distracted and amused by the parade of people in their at-home looks outdoors, so despite the smoke and the watering eyes it was all pretty amusing. I wasn't even bothered by the smoke that was now billowing out of the first story of the building.

Then I remembered Beth. Beth was the deaf, eighty-something-year-old woman who lived above me. She was 100 percent at home because she was at home 100 percent of the time and there was no way she heard the alarm or probably even noticed the smoke coming from the hallway into her apartment.

"Beth," I whispered to myself.

I looked around. The snow was coming down hard now, and there were still no firemen in sight. I didn't hear sirens in the distance, either. It occurred to me that there was a possibility that all the firefighters in the entire city were drinking eggnog and celebrating with their families. Who was working tonight? Jews? There are no Jewish firefighters.

Pulled by some unknown force, I started walking back toward the building.

"Dude! What are you doing?" screamed a bewildered Yoga Boobs from behind me. I didn't even turn around. I just kept walking. I was going to save Beth. She needed me. There was no way I was gonna let this old hoarder woman die on Christmas Eve. Not tonight. Not on my watch, Beth.

I'm a big dude, six foot three last time I checked, so I was able to jump my way up onto the lowest rung on the ladder hanging from the fire escape and pull myself up. It should be noted that this singular act was the first time I'd worked out since...literally ever. Superhuman strength made itself available to me in this fortuitous moment, miracles were taking place, and the presence of the Holy Spirit was felt by all who were witnessing me. Anyway, I got up to the fourth floor, wrapped my shirt around my hand, broke Beth's window from the outside, and climbed in. In addition to the smoke and fumes, it smelled like a library filled with cat shit on account of the cat shit and newspapers that filled Beth's disgusting apartment.

She was sitting in a chair in the far corner of the room. I couldn't tell if she was asleep or dead already. I ran over to her, leaping over a coffee table and two cats, and started to shake her violently.

"Beth!!!! Nooooo!!!!" I was screaming and coughing. The smoke was burning my lungs, and I could taste the ashes in my mouth. Shit was getting very real. Beth woke up and started screaming, too. For a couple seconds we were just staring into each other's eyes screaming at the top of our lungs. It was kind of magical.

I ripped her out of her chair and spun her around, her old tits bouncing all over the place. I lifted her into my arms like a wounded puppy. We were both still shrieking. As I ran downstairs through the smoke-filled stairwell I stumbled and nearly dropped her onto the floor. I burned my hand on the scalding-hot door handle to the outside, which by this point had been cooked by the flames coming from the floorboards. So instead, I kicked it in. The door flung open and we emerged onto the street.

It was all a blur, but looking back on it now, a severe shiver of fear shoots down my spine.

I carried Beth, triumphantly, out of the building just in time. People were clapping. I was a hero. It was like a mini 9/11, but instead of thousands perishing, I'd saved all of the lives that were in danger.

I let Beth down gently and with caution. She seemed pretty fucked up by the whole thing. I don't know if she totally understood what was going on, but then neither did I. Someone in the crowd told me that I'd only been in there for about a minute but it felt like a lifetime. I was just glad we weren't all dead. I was really hurting. I was spitting up black soot and it felt like I was dying.

The FDNY arrived and a ton of fire dudes ran into the lobby of the building. The woman who lived in the massive brownstone next door had come out to see what in the actual fuck was going on.

"What's going on? I heard sirens? Should I not go in my apartment?" she asked the crowd. She looked scared but not that scared because she was holding a glass of red wine in her left hand. I'd talked to her once before at the corner deli because I thought she was hot in a Lorraine Bracco–type way. I had no idea she lived in the swanky-as-fuck house next to my not-as-nice building.

"It's fine to go back into your house ma'am!" yelled a firefighter standing by his truck.

The scene on my street was really wild. All these people, scared, unsure whether their earthly possessions would be destroyed. Would we all be homeless on Christmas Eve? How savage would that be? Just a bunch of mostly stoned New Yorkers roaming the streets of the city in their pajamas all night long. Fighting through the snow for survival.

"The firemen just told me we can't go in for a few hours at least," Yoga Boobs announced to the group, looking devastated. "But they said it was just in the basement and the damages will be minimal."

"Why don't you all come warm up by my fireplace? I have plenty of space," Lorraine said to the group of maybe twelve of us.

"Great idea!" a voice from the crowd proclaimed.

"Let's do it," I said, looking into her eyes trying to see if she was DTF. I'm pretty sure she was because she smiled at me. Her teeth were very wine stained, which I'm very into.

The house was beautiful. Like, her brownstone was what would happen if a Restoration Hardware catalogue had unprotected sex with an issue of *Elle Decor* (I might not be straight). We all sat around the fire, and she poured us wine and brought out some food. Turns out, Lorraine was alone on Christmas Eve because she'd worked too hard at her finance job and her husband left her and took the kids. We drank more—she even had eggnog—we sang carols, and it quickly became the best Christmas Eve ever. Even Beth seemed to be loving it.

"I thought I was going to die tonight!" she announced to the crowd. We all loved Beth and were so happy that she was still with us. The odd mixture of people that were my neighbors were quickly becoming like family to me.

It also got very emotional around that fireplace. The combination of building fire drama and it being Christmas Eve and wine and everyone thinking about their families and what's important to them—it was a lot, and some people were crying as they shared Christmas stories. A few hours later, we were told that the building fire was put out and no one would *actually* be homeless, thank Jesus. Literally! Everyone shuffled themselves out of the apartment and back to our building. But I was too shaken up to leave, because despite my heroic efforts and my undeniable valor in the face of danger, I was scared, and I hadn't had time to process it all until that moment. Lorraine Bracco had drunk enough red wine and gobbled enough Valium to kill us all, so she didn't mind that I stayed, and I ended up in her arms by the fire, my head nestled against her extremely expensive and well-built fake breasts. I slept like a baby.

Was it worth risking my life for a woman that I barely knew, a woman who meant almost nothing to me? There is a famous quote I love that says "Be kind, for everyone you meet is fighting a hard battle," and that is something I always aspire to achieve.

Also, *none* of this happened. LOL. Like not at all. I would never, ever, ever go back into a burning building. Ever, for any reason whatsoever. I am so fucking selfish. There was actually an elderly woman who lived down the hall from me, but why would I save her from a fire? She was sooooo old and on the doorstep of death, why would I risk *this* gorgeous face for her? And most importantly here, I'm so fucking fat and Jewish that my weight and anxiety prohibit me from doing 99 percent of anything physical or potentially dangerous. So, climbing an old fire escape ladder and breaking a window with my hand would be completely out of the realm of possibilities of things I would ever, ever, ever do. Who am I, Jason Bourne? Would you have done this? *Don't even think about saying yes.*

CHILL ZONE #2

## HAIKU

thirty-one years old

still don't know what to do with

my arms when I sleep

## REGULAR POEM: HER

I saw her in the park

Her hair was dark, at peace

I saw her on the train

Her hands were small but graceful

I saw her in a shop

Her smile a warm mystery

I saw her on the street

Her skin was sweet and tan

I saw her at a park

My eyes were filled with joy

I would eat a full meal out of her asshole

Then miniaturize myself and crawl into her vagina

And sleep inside it like a satin pink slumber bag

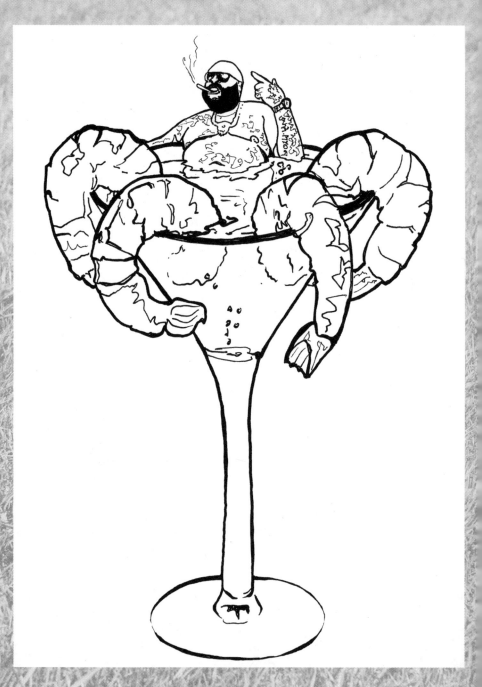

# THIS COUPON IS GOOD FOR:

# 3 BUTT GRABS

**(LIMITED TO ONE BUTT GRAB PER DAY)**

I'm very Jewish.

# JOSHUA

Hey diary (I think as a boy I'm supposed to call this a journal, but I don't want to, diary sounds way cooler)

I'm in bed and I can't sleep. Today was a pretty crazy day cause something really weird happened and I have been thinking about it a lot so I decided to write it down. I was in New Jersey at Grandma Roz's house watching The People's Court it was a great episode where this woman was suing her own son because he got mad at her and threw her TV out the window into a lake. Anyway I went to go into her bedroom because that's where she hides all the candy because my doctor says I'm overweight for my age and she was in the shower so I was just gonna sneak in and get some mini Milky Ways and then get out. So I went in and grabbed them but then she got out of the shower and as I was trying to escape she came out of the bathroom totally naked. I have seen naked chick's before because Teddy's older brother Jeff has great

porno videos that we watch when he's not home but most of girls in the videos have trimmed pain like a little strip and recently I downloaded some stuff on AOL where girls had no pubes at all. But this was wayyyyyyyyyyyyy different because grandma's bush went from her thighs all the way up past her private parts and all the way up to her bellybutton and out far on the edges like almost to her sides. She looked right at me and we locked eyes and then I ran out and hid in the garage for a while pretending to read some old magazines that she won't throw away.

We didn't talk about it afterwards we just pretended that it didn't happen and had dinner she made brisket. But now I'm at home and I can't stop thinking about it. It was more scary than anything I've ever seen including that movie Silence of the Lambs when that guy wags his tongue at the girl and is talking about beans that I watched at Doug's house (his parents are cool and actually let him watch R-rated movies) but I thought it would

go away by now, but now I'm thinking about it more. I would never tell anyone this but I'm really scared. It looked like a monster and even though I'm not scared of much anymore (i ride every rollercoaster at SixFlags) I feel really weird right now. I even just plugged in my night light which I haven't had to use since I was a little kid.

When will I stop thinking about this? what if it's forever??? I want to sleep but I'm afraid to close my eyes because I'll see it again. Who do i tell? I can't tell my parents that's so weird so maybe a teacher? Mr. Evans is cool, he'll understand I think. Might just keep it to myself. Ok, talk later.

## FAT JEW'S RECIPE FOR PRISON WINE

If for some reason you ever find yourself in prison, you're going to be sooooo bored, and you may also get shanked in the abdomen by a Guatemalan gang member with a shiv he made out of a carrot, but either way, you're going to want to get drunk. Hooch is hard to come by when the white man has you caged, so you'll probably have to go DIY. Rather than asking someone how to make prison booze and seeming wildly uncool, just memorize this recipe. (Actually, how do I get this book into prison libraries? Seriously, how does that work?) This recipe is very simple, and the result will get you drunk enough to forget that your life is in complete shambles and you've disgraced your entire family (unless you're in there for murdering them). Also, it's fun to make!

You'll need some supplies, some of which you can steal from the mess hall, some of which you can buy from the prison grocery store (I don't think that's what it's called), and some you'll have to get by...other means. Yes, like sucking a dick.

## What you'll need:

A big plastic bag that can be sealed

6–10 oranges

A huge can of fruit cocktail

40–60 sugar cubes

4–5 tablespoons of ketchup

1–3 pieces of bread

16 ounces of tap water—there is no sparkling in jail :(

1. Peel the oranges and toss them in the bag.
2. Dump the fruit cocktail in the bag.
3. Add the sugar.
4. Add the ketchup.
5. Add the bread (the yeast helps the fermentation process).
6. Add the water.
7. Seal the bag and beat the shit out of it with your fists.
8. Store the bag somewhere warm or pour warm water over it several times a day.
9. After 5–7 days, it's ready to drink.
10. Serves 3–4. Smells like a corpse filled with farts and orange juice, pairs well with a nice piece of fish and some rice pilaf— just kidding, you're in jail.
11. It will seriously fuck you up, though.

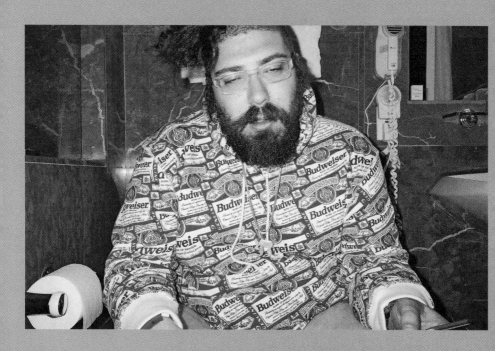

# 10.

# I PUKED ON MY GRANDPA. WHAT DID YOU DO TODAY?

o say that my existence was fueled by cocaine in most of 2009 would be an understatement. Maybe that sounds really dark, but it wasn't. It was actually really fucking fun. I was living alone in my parents' apartment on the Upper West Side. They'd just moved to New Zealand for a year because my dad, a physician, was taking a sabbatical/having a midlife crisis. Thankfully that meant leaving me in their duplex.

Within an hour of my parents moving out I had these two bull-dyke lesbians I knew help me move all of the valuable possessions (art, sculpture, heirlooms) that belonged to my mom and dad into a storage unit I'd rented. The debauchery I was going to bring upon their home would inevitably destroy everything it came in contact with. I'm talking my framed baby pictures being used as a coke mirror level of disrespect. I was living carefree and rent-free, and I'd always have my degenerate friends over to watch me be ridiculous and irresponsible. I filled one entire room of the apartment with sand and made it look like a shitty beach. I used their pool table as the dining room table for just about every meal, and I primarily peed in the sinks.

In addition to inviting my group of friends over to the apartment every night, I'd also invite this douche canoe named Keith, who I never would've never hung out with but for the fact that he was constantly in possession of a shit ton of drugs. It was a wonderful time in my life.

One night while we were chilling at the house, doing a few lines of coke off my parents' wedding album, Keith suggested that we head to a loft party in Chinatown. The party sounded awesome, because when you're coked up literally everything sounds awesome. If someone had invited me to look at their garbage can at that moment, I would've happily gone. When we got there I immediately struck up a conversation with this girl named Lil' Website, who I kind of knew from Facebook. I'm not kidding, that

 was her name, for real. She looked like Linda Perry, the lead singer of 4 Non Blondes. White skin, blonde dreads, heavy makeup. Lil' Website was telling me about her job, working for this company that made clothing for Goth babies.

"Are they actually Goth babies?" I ask.

"What? Yes. Of course there are Goth babies. Every baby I know is a Goth baby," she replied, a bit too angrily.

"Come on. That can't be true."

"It's a huge market. I just came back from a children's clothing trade show and there is so much competition in the space now."

"As in, multiple Goth baby companies?" I asked, accompanied with an eye roll.

"You are so *out of the loop*, Fat Jew!" she exclaimed, basically screaming.

It was at this exact moment that I realized that she, like me, was also coked the fuck up. I could tell by the way she was breathing and the tone of her voice. And when you're high on cocaine, nothing makes you happier than someone else who is also high.

> **Sidenote**
>
> If you've ever done coke, you know that it makes you talk at least three times faster than normal. So as you read this next bit of dialogue, please read it three times as fast as you normally read. It's okay if you miss some of the words, or even if you miss the entire point, just read frantically. *That is what it's like when you are on coke!* Nothing that anyone is saying really matters.

"Do you have any coke?" I asked.

"Oh yeah. Lots. Let's go to the bathroom, blow some lines, and then go to my current fave place in NYC, Dave and Buster's."

"I really like this plan."

So that is what we did. Bathroom, coke, cab, Dave, Buster. Once we were there we saddled up at the bar, which was wedged between the Skee-Ball and the fake casino, and got into a deeeeeep conversation.

"There are no good places in NYC to get a tattoo and eat dinner at the same time," I said as I took a bite of my Miso-Glazed Salmon. "It seems so obvious, and I'm honestly not sure why this is an untapped market," I offered.

"No. No. You're totally fucking right. That's genius." Lil' Web's mind is blown right now, as much by my business acumen as she was by the Black Bean Veggie Burger she was eating. Dave and Buster's does not fuck around with its menu.

"Right? Like I just thought of that, and I was like, holy shit, that's fucking genius," I added.

"Or, or, or, let's start a social network! Mark Zuckerberg did it, so why couldn't we do it too? Facebook is *fucking lame.*"

"No, you're right, dude"—I was so coked up—"but, imagine this: breast implants...*with wifi in them.*"

"Should we go to the aquarium together tomorrow? *I haven't been in so long and I love how the walruses have mustaches.*"

"Yes. Yes. Yes," I replied, although I would have said yes to literally anything in order to have sex with her.

"Should we do more coke?" she offered.

"Yes," I replied.

"Yesssssssssssss!" she yelled, our faces now close enough together that I could see the ring of chapped skin around her lips, which for some reason I didn't find gross.

"Yes. Yes. Yes." I couldn't stop saying yes.

I definitely need to spruce up a bit so I was stoked that she had more. After a few lines each, we made out for a couple minutes (coke makes you want to fuck). Did a few more lines after we made out and then exited the tiny bathroom, back into the arcade, which seemed to have escalated into overdrive while we were gone. Teens were screaming and playing those games where you dance really fast. I think we were in the middle of a birthday party.

"I fucking hate everyone at this party," she said.

In the interest of my penis, I decided to take this relationship to the next level.

"I fucking hate everyone everywhere, so I'm so down to leave. Let's get out of here," I said, and we were out of there, my brain and heart desperately trying to process the additional chemicals they had just been hit with.

Lil' Website and I were out of our minds. She told me that she wanted to "fuck my face," which sounded like a great idea, so we headed home to my place, which was exactly eighty-three blocks from the bar we were sitting in. Which at the time seemed totally walkable. Plus we needed time to hash out our future boob wifi business.

The details are fuzzy, but at some point on the way home, I think we got into a huge argument about whether Nazis were the most fashionable group of people of all time. I honestly don't know which side I was arguing, which is insane considering members of my family were killed in the Holocaust. But that's coke for you. I do remember fingering Lil' Web up against a Dumpster, stealing some heads of lettuce being delivered to a grocery store, and her screaming at me and angrily getting into a taxi. No biggie. I walked the rest of the way by myself, stopping for a delicious street gyro along the way, before returning to my parents' place.

As soon as I walked in the door, I took off my pants and stumbled past my parents' bedroom, where I'd been staying since they moved out. The chemicals in my system and my parents' empty apartment at five a.m. combined to create a powerful nostalgia, so I walked into my childhood room and laid down.

From the top bunk of my bunk bed, staring at the ceiling, my heart fucking exploding out my chest, I could see just enough sunlight spilling through the blinds to give me anxiety about how late/early it was. I recapped the previous twelve hours of poor decisions and wondered why my fingers smelled so strange. My stomach started making a crazy noise. I started breathing heavily, leaned over, and threw up approximately three gallons of sewage.

It felt *amazing*. Like I'd exorcised the demons of the night. Like I had cleared the way toward a cleaner, healthier lifestyle. It was easily one of the greatest feelings of my entire life to this day. And then the light flipped on. Standing there, in some old-timey striped pajamas with giant plastic buttons, covered in the puke, was my grandfather.

"*Are you fucking kidding me?*" he screamed in his thick Russian accent.

I started screaming like a seven-year-old girl. Turns out, he'd been staying in the apartment for a few days, but no one had told me, and I hadn't noticed him! Apparently there was a loud noise coming from the air-conditioner in the guest room, so he decided to go into my old bedroom, with no idea that I was going to show up, coked up and filled with bad gyro, and puke onto him.

After my grandfather screamed at me ("You are a giant bearded infant!") and expressed to me how pathetic my generation was (apparently we need to stop spending all our time "jacking off" to Facebook, which he calls Spacebook), he picked up the bedsheet and did his best to wipe himself off. He stormed out to go take a shower, and that was the last I saw of him that night.

The next afternoon I woke up and mentally recapped the horrible events of the previous evening. Then I masturbated in near silence because I wasn't sure if my grandpa was still in the house, and I knew we'd gone through enough in the last few hours. Finally around three p.m. I climbed out of bed to face the day and to try to sweep up the pieces of my shattered life. Grandpa was in the kitchen eating Good & Plenty candies and reading a newspaper, both of which are old-timey and gross to the max but also so adorable and cute. I broke the awkward silence: "If you want to vomit on me later, you totally can." We both laughed.

I sat down on his lap and began kissing his neck, he mumbled something like "Your skin is soft like a woman I knew in Korea during the war." There was so much heat between us, and I felt like my body was on fire. *Guys, just kidding. Holy fuck, imagine if that actually happened. I wish I could have seen your face when you thought I was hooking up with my own grandfather.*

What actually happened was that I sat down at the table with him, we drank a cup of coffee, and I invited him to do something that I knew he wanted to do: go to the off-track betting place on Lexington Avenue. We spent the rest of the day watching guys with mustaches blow their kids' community college funds on horses with names like Wallpaper's Wish and Let's Go Dancing!

My grandfather and I didn't talk much, and there was something comforting about it. After a long night of screaming lots of nothing at other people, it felt great to just be comfortable with someone in total silence. I think it was the first (and perhaps only) time I actually appreciated my strong, hard-working, silent-type, immigrant grandfather.

"Honestly, I'm really sorry that I threw up on you like that," I said, looking up at him. I meant it.

My grandfather then turned toward me and stared for what felt like an eternity. The look on his face made me scared I'd brought this whole thing up again.

"Don't," he said quietly.

"Don't what?" I was confused.

"You and your goddam stupid generation. Always apologizing for everything. A bunch of pussies. Every last one of you."

"What are you talking about? I'm just saying I'm sorry."

"Well, stop. You messed up. You puked on me. You didn't mean to do it. So stop apologizing. So what? You puked on me. It's not the first time I've been puked on, and I've puked on people before."

"Okay?"

"Also, you insult me by apologizing. I'm not a pussy. I can handle a little puke. I've seen shit that was way worse that that... way...worse. So grow some balls, be a man, and own the fact that you couldn't handle your shit last night."

"So don't apologize, then?"

"You're a fucking idiot. Just like your father. Who do you like in this next one?" he asked, looking back up at the screen, which displayed the names of the horses in the next heat.

"Pot-of-Gold?" I replied, having no idea who to go with.

"There you go. Now we're talking."

11.

# THE ELEVEN COMMANDMENTS OF NOT BEING THE WORST PERSON EVER

This book has already taught you so many things, am I right? Yes, I'm right. Now, granted, most of what you've learned is based on mistakes I've made and the collateral life damage that my decisions have caused, but having me as sort of a bizarre moronic older brother who paves the way for you by doing unimaginably stupid shit and showing you how *not* to live is definitely beneficial to your life.

In case you weren't aware, I was raised in New York City and attended private school, because my parents are extremely wealthy doctors. (JK JK JK—They weren't that rich; they are incredibly sensible Jews who eat seafood at diners, so gross.) Manhattan private schools are the #1 breeding ground for over-privileged douche canoes whose parents are constantly traveling for business and thus are basically raised by Trinidadian nannies and ATM cards with unlimited funds. After college I traveled the world (hid from the real world) and studied horrendous people around the globe, immersing myself into their culture, living among them to observe them on a daily basis. Ravers in Norway. Frat boys in Australia. DJs in Los Angeles. Fishermen in China. In a study conducted solely by me, I've met over 65 percent of the worst people on the planet.

Basically, I'm an *asshole anthropologist*.

I have finally decided to use my findings for the greater good, to take all this compiled knowledge and use it to help the world. Whether you are fifteen years old and have your life ahead of you, or fifty and just realizing that you might actually be the worst, here is a guide to helping you avoid pitfalls along the way. I can't tell you what you should be doing, but I certainly can tell you what you shouldn't.

If I remember the Bible correctly, Moses comes down from a mountain holding two giant stone tablets, and etched into those tablets are the rules that form the entire basis of the Jewish religion. Now imagine me, clad in white linen, emerging from a strip club off the side of a highway on a Thursday morning, holding two tablets of my own that read:

## FJ'S 11 COMMANDMENTS

### I.
### DO NOT EXPRESS YOURSELF THROUGH A HAT.

There are so many wonderful ways to let the world know that you are the unique and special snowflake that your mother always said you were: Sing, dance, get a tattoo of a gorilla wearing sunglasses while surfing, become one of those people who manually masturbates animals to collect their semen for research—*I don't care what you do to separate yourself from the crowd. Anything* but wearing a stupid hat. You think it makes you seem fun, right? Or fashionable? No. It just makes people hate you.

*Exceptions: The Kentucky Derby, orthodox Jews, court jesters at Renaissance fairs.*

# II.
## DON'T TALK ABOUT YOUR JOB.

As you get older, you will find that your life becomes increasingly devoid of social interaction and joy, and you will spend exorbitant amounts of time working and learning what a mortgage is (I have *no idea*, and it's been explained to me like three times). As much as you want to be like "no way, brahhh, I'll never be defined by my job!" you most definitely will. At some point during your journey you will be forced to find something, anything, to do for a living. It might be something that you are passionate about, or maybe you will hate it. But you will have to actually work. Or just be homeless, which is very chill if you're fine with smelling like butthole.

Most people just end up getting jobs, though. Even the really crazy people. I know some dudes who used to smoke formaldehyde (yes, the liquid you store human brains in, and yes, you can smoke it) four times a week and would try to rip their own penises off for fun, who now, in their thirties, have found careers.

Remember when I referred to life as "your journey"? LOLOLOLOL that was terrible.

Obviously I encourage you to follow your dreams and dive in headfirst. But please, please, please, even though you are way into your job, even though it consumes 90 percent of your life and thoughts, and even if your job is "cool," don't make it the thing you talk about the most. Nobody wants to hear about it, I fucking swear. People are generally polite and will definitely sit and listen to a story about how some guy you work with is always eating tuna for lunch, but in their hearts and brains they will be picturing a scenario where they are pushing you into some shrubs or off a massive cliff to your death!

*Exception: Leonardo DiCaprio. That guy's job involves sleeping with sixteen women born in the former Yugoslavia simultaneously.*

*Leo, tell me all about it and, please, don't ever stop.*

# III.
## DON'T DO COCAINE.

Cocaine is the greatest gift the world has ever received. It is responsible for some of its greatest art, legendary ideas, and most phenomenal stories. Imagine Charlie Sheen driving on the PCH in 1992 in a convertible, doing key bumps, not looking at the road, with a girl definitely named Nikki who had rock hard breast implants and hates her dad sitting shotgun, blasting George Michael and laughing hysterically at nothing in particular. That would be *amazing*. But guess what? That's not you. (Unless Sheen is reading this, in which case NVMD.)

Instead, you're probably in the bathroom of a holiday party (pick any holiday) with some guy you barely know named Jeff talking about how *Under the Tuscan Sun* with Diane Lane was actually really good. Don't know that movie? Doesn't matter. It sucks. The point is that cocaine will get you into an overly intense conversation about some shit you absolutely don't care about.

On top of that, cocaine leaves your breath smelling like a corpse filled with lo mein and makes you a bad listener, a loud talker, and a constant nodder, because you are saying yes to anything people are telling you.

I'm not a doctor, but cocaine can't kill you. I mean, I guess it can, but you have to be seriously rich and doing a truly insane amount of it. The real danger in cocaine lies in how much of a monster it makes you, so just don't.

*Exception: You are under a waterfall on a cliff at sunset in South America. Go for it.*

# IV.
## DO NOT BE OVERLY POSITIVE.

This is exactly why I live in New York and not Los Angeles. A large number of people who reside in LA are constantly positive, and I believe that the person who is constantly positive will be the first one to murder you. They are not to be trusted. Anyone who is like "it's all good, brahhh, namaste" needs to *nama-stay the fuck away from me.*

*Exception: When you are basically being crushed by life and need to surround yourself with overly positive deluded people who will make you feel not so horrendous. You have six months tops to snap out of it, or you will get murdered.*

# V.
## DON'T USE A DORITOS BAG AS A CONDOM.

You may be blackout drunk and not want to go all the way to a store to buy condoms, but you just have to. Or just hang out with her and talk. From experience, I can tell you: Don't tie a Doritos bag around your penis and secure it with a rubber band. It will chafe your penis and make it red, like E.T.'s glowing finger. Trust me.

*Exceptions: None.*

## VI.
### DON'T MAKE MOVIE QUOTES YOUR PRIMARY COMEDY SOURCE.

Your ability to quote a funny line from a movie does not, by extension, make you funny. I stopped having sex with a girl because she used the Borat voice twice, non-ironically.

*Exceptions: None.*

# VII.
## DON'T SAY WORDS IN OTHER LANGUAGES IN THE ACCENT OF THAT LANGUAGE.

Nothing is worse than a white girl who once traveled to Barcelona for ten days ordering lunch at a Spanish restaurant and rolling the fuck out of her rs like "I'll have the empahhhhhnahhh-das with rrrrrrrropo vieja."

You know who does this all time? *Alex Trebek.*

Contestant: "What are the Andes Mountains?"

Alex Trebek: I'm sorry, the correct response was 'What is *Ma-chu Pi-cchu.*'"

Even if you speak the language fluently, go easy. Or just order in that language. Nothing wrong with you being worldly and bilingual. Just don't be an asswipe.

*Exception: Sofia Vergara.*

# VIII.
## DON'T BE AFRAID TO EAT
## AT STRIP CLUBS.

Strip club food has a bad rap, and deservedly so. For years it was wings, tater skins, hush puppies, and pizza kept under a heat lamp. But times have changed. Strip club chefs are taking bold and daring risks in the kitchen, and it's producing some phenomenal results. There is now a strip club open in Portland that is entirely vegan; the quinoa-stuffed bell pepper is a revelation. In New York City, Rick's Cabaret in midtown is serving a Caesar salad that is a tour de force on the palate. They are making their croutons in house using ciabatta baked fresh each morning in Brooklyn. Down in Miami at E11even, the caprese salad will legitimately whisk you away to southern Italy with its incredibly fresh buffalo mozzarella and sliced heirloom tomatoes. Strip clubs have become a destination for culinary delights. It's time for us as a country to abandon the old prejudices and embrace the new wave of gastronomic genius emerging from these establishments. Don't be afraid any longer.

*Exceptions: Strip clubs in Tampa Bay. The food at those is insane.
I ate a pizza with pineapple on it while drunk at one and my
anus was an explosive volcano. A volcanus?*

# IX.
## DON'T AGGRESSIVELY TALK ABOUT SEX ALL THE TIME, UNLESS YOU WANT PEOPLE TO THINK YOU'RE GAY.

This applies to members of both sexes. Anytime you talk about sex constantly and are overtly aggressive about it, it makes you seem really really gay. If I ask you how your date last night went and your response is "Dude, I used my fuck rod to slam her right in the pussy slot!" you sound like a guy who has never had sex with an actual woman before. When you tell me that you "tackled a slam pig and stuffed her axe wound," I assume that your actual goal is having anal sex with men, because no actual straight men speak to each other like that.

*Exception: Dan Bilzerian.*

## X.
## DON'T TALK SO LOUD.

S eriously, you are screaming. All the time.

*Exceptions: None.*

## XI.
### DON'T EAT SUSHI AT A GAS STATION.

Trust me. Trust me. Please trust me. It seems pretty obvious that eating sushi at a convenience store is not something a thinking person would do. But I've done it. And it did not go well. So I felt it best to just put it out there, in print.

*Exceptions: Meth addicts.*

# READING SUCKS. HERE'S A COMIC BOOK.

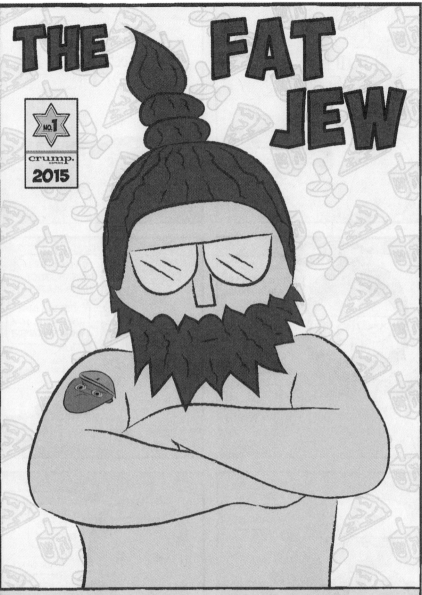

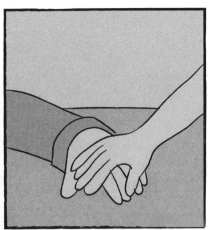

THE FAT JEW TRAVELS THROUGH TIME
AND STOPS TERRIBLE THINGS
FROM HAPPENING

till too tired to read more words? Fuck reading! Let's enjoy these tasty photos of me wearing a vest and bikini briefs made entirely out of beef jerky!

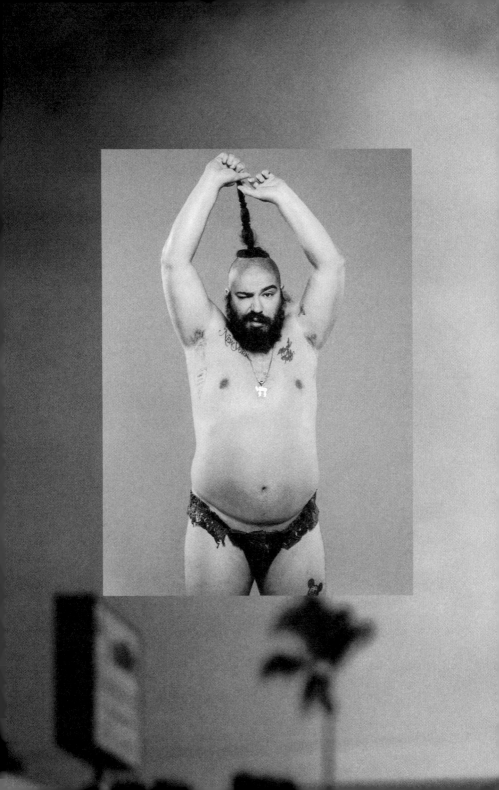

# 13.
# HOOKER
# *BRAVEHEART*

People have a negative view of prostitutes. I get that. They bang people for money. But I know a lot more hookers than most, and I've been able to form a different opinion of professional sex workers in my time on Earth. I know what you're thinking. *Why would such a handsome, sexy, creative, talented specimen need to pay for sex?* But my hooker proclivity isn't only about actual sex. Prostitutes can do so many things besides suck dicks, fuck dicks, and pretend to like you. You just need to give them a chance. You can hire a working girl to do any number of random tasks, sexual or otherwise.

It's really so much fun. And then you can still have sex with them if you feel like it.

Maybe it's because I wasn't born with any human emotions or maybe it's that I've become so desensitized because of pornography and strip clubs, but I don't get excited by standard or normal sexual encounters anymore. It just doesn't cut it for me. There needs to be more to the story than just my penis entering something. Therein lies my issue: Most humans aren't on my level of deviance. You can't just ask someone you've just met if they'd mind dressing up in a JonBenét Ramsey outfit and playing out a murder fantasy that you've cooked up. That takes time, nurturing, and a mutual respect for one another. And I'm not really into work or effort when it comes to sex. Which is why I rely on professionals. You can pay them to do basically *anything*. I've paid hookers come over and cook me pasta, clip my toenails, and watch *Mean Girls* with me. Not to get too psychological, but it's very interesting how they react when approached about these types of activities. You would think they'd be overjoyed to not have my Shrek-like body on top of them thrusting my champagne-cork shaped penis inside of them, but some almost prefer sex to alternative activities. If you want to fuck them, fine, but ask one to organize your spice rack and suddenly they think you're a murderer and want to leave. It's fifty-fifty.

A couple of New Year's Days ago, I was recovering from a hellish night of molly/vodka/coke/weed/Xanax/coke/weed/Xanax/ Indian food by lying in bed and eating a gigantic bowl of pasta with the Indian leftovers mixed in. As I flipped through the channels I stumbled upon *Braveheart*, which was playing on TNT or some other shitty channel that actually isn't shitty because it basically only played *Braveheart*. My relationship with Mel Gibson had gone through a very rocky period in the prior few years (as he transitioned from the hunk with flowing hair in *Lethal Weapon* who I wanted to be best friends with to an anti-Semitic monster), but I still had so much love for *Braveheart*, partially because of the themes of honor, loyalty, and the desire for personal freedom, but mostly because it has dudes on horses wielding axes that are on fire. Through the cloud of hangover, I, like Shawn Carter, had a moment of clarity. Inspiration swept through me like an electrical charge. I leapt up, scattering penne across the bed, grabbed my iPhone, and called my fave service.

I had them send over two escorts to my apartment. This particular company guarantees their girls in under an hour or you get to have sex with them for free, which is the only thing darker than having sex for money. By the way, that's not a joke—it's literally the stated HR policy. So basically the girls are never ever ever ever late. Meanwhile, I spent the next thirty minutes getting things organized.

Once my place looked and smelled less like a doodoo diaper filled with chicken tikka masala, I showered and posted up by the doorway with my front door left slightly ajar. The buzzer rang.

"Who is it?" I asked in an overly friendly voice that ironically sounded murder-y.

"Us," a voice said through the intercom.

"Us who?" I replied in my most coy voice.

"Are you fuckin' kidding, buddy—"

"Okay, yeah yeah, I'm kidding." I pressed the buzzer. "Come on up."

"Hey there, big fella," the shorter one said as she walked into my place. She looked like a cross between Danny DeVito and Rhea Perlman. So...not hot, but fun looking? (Side note: Ironically,

I did fuck Danny DeVito and Rhea Perlman's daughter IRL. Maybe I can cover that in my second book. Also, Mom, if you're reading this, which is fucked up to begin with, IRL is Internet slang for "in real life.") The other girl was medium sized with big tits and a birthmark on her neck.

"I appreciate what you're going for with the whole big fella routine, but that's really not necessary," I replied. She stared back at me blankly.

"I'm Crystal," said the medium girl, who was hotter than the first one. She reminded me of Brooke Burke, but more hooker-y. She also didn't look anything like Brooke Burke. She looked more like Brooke Hogan. Actually, she also kind of looked like Paul Hogan.

"Cool. I'm Josh. Make yourself comfortable in my humble abode," I said.

I would never actually say "abode" in normal conversation, but the nervous excitement just got to me in that moment.

**Sidenote**

### NOW LET ME PAINT YOU A PICTURE WITH WORDS (BECAUSE THIS IS A BOOK):

At the time, I was living in this tiny fucking basement apartment on West 15th Street. It was basically a bed, a chair, the smallest kitchen imaginable, and a shelf. The bathroom was so bad I could never do it justice. The one thing this extremely small/extremely expensive apartment had going for it was an outdoor space. The holy grail of NYC living. The unit had a little backyard with a grill, which is very chill for NYC. A real luxury. The outdoor space was also a game changer in terms of cigarette smoking.

Most people who smoke cigarettes don't understand the struggle of living in the city and having to leave your home and your building to get out to the street, just to smoke. It's fucking terrible. The struggle is very real.

*Very fucking real.* I mean, sometimes in New York you can get away with just smoking out your window, but then there's always this one neighbor who keeps complaining about the smell, and then the super gets on you about it, which is not that great, so you stop for a while and go back to walking out to the street three hundred times a day to smoke, until it gets freezing again and you get lazy so you start to just smoke out of the window again, but then that dirty hoarder neighbor lady starts to complain again…you get the idea.

Anyway, this apartment didn't have anything going for it but the outdoor space, but you can see how important that space was to me.

OK. Back to New Year's Day. So there we were, the three of us, just two hookers and me. Crystal was very talkative and nice. But the DeVito one was getting less attractive every time she opened her mouth.

"So this is a shithole, huh?"

"Why, yes, it is. Thank you for noticing," I replied.

"You have a poster of Usher standing shirtless in the rain? Are you gay?"

"Dawn, don't be fuckin' rude." Crystal quickly added, "There's outdoor space over here."

"Oh…excuse me, Crystal, I wasn't aware that you and fat John over here shared a deep love for organic gardening and local produce," Dawn said.

"Um, it's Fat Josh, actually." I smiled.

"Whatever. Can we do this? I don't get paid by the hour, so the sooner we get you off, the sooner I can go home. My Netflix queue is craaaaaaazy long right now."

"Speaking of Netflix, I'm going to need you both to take a look at these," I said, handing them both pieces of printer paper.

I had prepared and printed out the script for the epic battle scene from *Braveheart*, including the "They'll never take our freedom" speech. I'd also run down to the pharmacy on the corner and bought a kids' paint set, so I could recreate the iconic blue and white face paint from the film. I knew I wouldn't be able to climax if we didn't address all of the scene's details.

"What the fuck am I supposed to do with this?" Dawn asked, leafing through the script.

"It's a scene from *Braveheart*. I want you two to act out this battle for me, topless. Just put on this blue and white face paint and then we can get this going," I said, handing them each a spatula sword from my kitchen.

"Oh, hell no," Dawn said. "I don't have time for this shit."

"I don't understand."

"I'm not doing this. Can't I just fuck you and go?"

"You don't even need to fuck me," I clarified. "Just put this paint on your face, take your top off, ride me like a horse, and read the lines. Then I'll pay you and you can go home to your house, which is apparently much nicer than this place."

"Nah. This shit is too weird for me. I'm breaking out. Crystal? You stayin' here with this freaky-ass white boy?"

"Yeah," Crystal said.

"He's probably gonna murder you. Or cry. I can't do the crying, girl. No way. I'm out."

"I'm not going to murder anybody. What are you talking about?"

"Okay, well, the whole thing is freaking me out. I'm done," Dawn said. She was getting agitated. and I needed to find a way to get her to stay.

"I'm sorry. So you'd rather fuck me, a complete stranger that looks like this," I said, gesturing to myself, "than act out a scene from an incredible movie? How does that make any sense?"

"I'm a *hooker*. I ain't no *actress*."

Dawn was very pissed.

"Dawn, just calm down," Crystal chimed in. "Just go home, babe. I'll be fine. I can handle this on my own."

"If I leave you here and you don't text me in the next hour, I'm-a call the police and tell them you got murdered on Fifteenth Street. You got that, fat man?"

"Jesus. Yes. No one is going to get hurt," I assured her.

"I'm fine, Dawn. I'm fine."

Dawn did leave, thank God. She was a fucking nightmare. Bye, Dawn, GTFO. When the door shut behind her, Crystal turned to me and smiled.

"I love this movie."

"Okay. Wow." I was shocked. "Wow. I mean, I was thinking I'd be lucky if you even knew what *Braveheart* was, but you *love* it? Fuck yeah. I'm a huge Mel Gibson fan. I find anti-Semitic people to be really fascinating."

"So you want me to play William Wallace?"

"Yes, exactly. That would be great. Just go in the bathroom, put on this face paint, and come out when you're ready. Here is a picture of Mel in full makeup so you can match it to the best of your ability," I said, handing Crystal her props. "Doesn't have to be perfect. Just do your best."

Crystal came out of the bathroom in full character paint. Her face looked amazing. Topless, she mounted me like the battle horse I was and began her performance:

**CRYSTAL:**

Sons of Scotland, I am William Wallace.

**ME:**

William Wallace is seven feet tall.

**CRYSTAL:**

Yes, I've heard. Kills men by the hundreds, and
if he were here he'd consume the English with
fireballs from his eyes and bolts of lightning from
his *arse*! [I laughed here.] I *am* William Wallace.
And I see a whole army of my countrymen here
in defiance of tyranny. You have come to fight as
free men, and free men you are. What would you
do without freedom? Will you fight?

**ME:**

Fight? Against that? No, we will run, and we
will live.

**CRYSTAL:**

Aye, fight and you may die. Run and you'll
live—at least a while. And dying in your beds
many years from now, would you be willing to
trade all the days from this day to that for one
chance, just one chance to come back here and
tell our enemies that they may take our lives,
but they'll *never take our freedom*!!!

**BOTH:**

Alba gu bra! Scotland forever!

At that point she hopped off of my back, threw me the
extra spatula that Dawn had left on my bed, and started sword
fighting me as if I were the enemy. Crystal was an amazing
actress. Like, she fucking nailed it. I was in awe of her talent
and commitment to the role. Needless to say, the sword play
eventually devolved into wrestling, which ultimately became
another type of *sword* play, if you get my drift. I mean that we
fucked.

After we were done (two minutes), we just laid there in my
bed. Our embrace was much more intimate that you'd imagine
a hooker/John postcoital moment to be. I honestly think
she'd been turned on by the whole scenario just as much as
I had.

"I got into NYU Tisch School of the Arts acting program, but
had to turn it down because they didn't give me enough financial
aid and my family couldn't pay for it." Crystal sighed.

"Holy shit. Are you serious? I was gonna say, your acting is really good."

"Yeah. I guess I've always had it in me, to be a great actor. Just wasn't really given a chance. I like what I do, though. It's really fun, when it's fun. Today was fun."

We shared a laugh. Then I leaned in and kissed her on the mouth. She recoiled.

"Um...No thanks, Josh. This was nice, but I don't kiss."

"Totally get it. I may have misread the situation here."

"It's fine. No harm done. I'll leave you my number when I go. Call me anytime you want to do this kind of thing again. It was really great to flex that muscle again. I miss it."

Paying my new scene partner to fuck me and then watching her leave in hooker heels was an odd experience. Crystal was more than just a hire for me. I felt like I'd made a new friend.

I called my cousin who is an acting agent and told him about my friend Crystal who was in between agents. I went on and on about how I saw her in this avant-garde stage production of *Braveheart* and that she just blew me away. My douchebag cousin only agreed to meet with her after I told him that she was smoking hot and had big funbags.

I don't know what happened to Crystal exactly. She must have changed her phone number, because the one I have for her doesn't work. I just tried it. I guess I could follow up with my cousin, but I owe him two hundred bucks from a bet I lost, so I don't really want to check in. But...I *swear* I saw Crystal on a New York State Lotto commercial last month. I'm 99 percent sure it was her. She looked great, and I feel like I am in some way responsible for her turning her life around.

Hope you are happy with whatever you are doing, Crystal. I'll never forget your performance. And if you still see Dawn, tell her to go fuck herself.

## HAIKU

Please don't hold the door

if i'm like 12 feet away

I HATE THAT WEIRD JOG

# JOSHUA

On Saturday I woke up early like always and ate a candy bar that I hid under my bed. It was a Milky Way which is my favrite even though my friend Mike said it looked like a piece of doodie. The house was quiet so I went to the living room but I heard scary sounds from my mommy and daddys room like when our cat Toby tried to fight grandmas dog and I got scared. But I wanted to be brave so I went into the room to save mommy but daddy was on top of her and they were yelling at each other and mashing their bodies together and daddy saw me and told me to get out and I cried.

I went to Dr. Levine, my orthodontist today to get braces which is amazing because Brian has braces and he goes to Knicks games all the time and has a hypercolor t-shirt and he smells like a magazine my dad reads and he's popular. But at the orthodontist, I started reading Highlights magazine and my mom who took me told me that Highlights is a magazine for younger children, and that I should ride Time or something and took Highlights away. I told her Time is the most boring magazine ever and I told her to leave me alone and asked her if it was that time of the month which I heard on Married with Children and she asked me if I wanted a spanking. So I had to sit and read a time Magazine article about cows I hated it so much and then the doctor came out and brought me into his office and I cried. I don't think I will ever forgive mom for that ever.

# WHITE GIRL ROSÉ SANGRIA

As many of you may know, I make a rosé that is fucking delicious. One of my fave things to do on a hot summer day when I'm spending time with friends is to make some delicious rosé sangria!!!! (Sorry, that was way too much excitement.)

*Here is what you will need:*

## INGREDIENTS

3 bottles White Girl rosé (don't use any other rosé or the taste will be horrendous)

3 cups Grand Marnier

3 cups strawberries (sliced thin)

1 cup water

1 cup mint leaves

1 peach, chopped

1 cup of halved green grapes

1 cup sugar

1. Pour all the ingredients into a pitcher, mix with a spoon, and drink.

2. Drink.

3. Since I tripled all the ingredient amounts, this potion will actually turn you into a white girl. Regardless of your race or gender, you will immediately start speaking very loud (borderline screaming) and saying things like, "OH MY GOD, THAT IS RIDICULOUS!!!" to things that aren't really ridiculous, and smoking a Marlboro Light cigarette while saying, "I NEVER SMOKE. THIS IS SOOOOOO CRAZY THAT I AM DOING THIS."

1. The alcohol was tripled. Make a questionable sexual decision: you aren't responsible for your actions at that point!

# THIS COUPON IS GOOD FOR:

**ONE**

HJ → BJ

**Upgrade**

**OR**

BJ → HJ

**DOWNGRADE**

THIS COUPON IS GOOD FOR:

ONE FREE

FroYo!

*(SIZE SMALL WITH TWO TOPPINGS)*

AT NEAREST FROZEN YOGURT SHOP

# 15.

# 2080 IS GOING TO BE AWFUL(LY AMAZING)

To the Readers of My Book *Money Pizza Respect*,

I have no idea if this letter will actually find its way into the first printing of my book, but I certainly hope it does. It is the year 2080. I am in the future and I recently met a man on a digibeach who was way chill. Naturally we engaged in a datamosh and started smoking this killer thumbdrive that he had smuggled in from the country of Florida...

Wait, fuck, I just realized that none of that makes any sense to you. How do I explain this so that your undeveloped past brain can understand? OK, here goes: Met a guy, we were smoking drugs, hanging out, and talking, and he told me he was a time traveler (he had badass sunglasses on and a trench coat so he definitely looked like the type of guy who could surf through time and space) and in exchange for some bitcoins (now the national currency, obviously) he agreed to deliver this letter to the editor of my book in the year 2015. So if you're reading this, then I guess he was successful, but there's no real way for me to know unless I can somehow miraculously find a copy of that book. Paper books were outlawed decades ago. All the old books were used as toilet paper before humans eventually phased out buttholes altogether in 2069.

It was challenge for me to even write this letter as I haven't actually physically written anything in years. In fact, it took me several weeks to get a pen, which I was only able to obtain because a friend of mine works for the Museum of Pasts and was able to put one on loan from their When Humans Used Their Hands exhibit. Correct, nobody has really used their hands in years. Some people even had their hands replaced with awesome things, like claws, mirrors, torgens (it's like a phone but better). I know this one guy named Fif who has titanium dildo hands.

You might be asking yourself how much could really change in sixty-five years, and the answer is absolutely *everything*. If you are reading this in 2015, then just think about sixty years before this moment right now, people thought cigarettes had essential vitamins and minerals and doctors were prescribing them to pregnant women to relieve stress. Most people thought that radio would always be their primary form of entertainment. Cars were projectile death machines. It was the fucking Stone Age compared to 2015...

So, as you might imagine, in the future, the planet is really, really fucked up. Antarctica is completely melted, the Middle East has been on fire (no, like actually on fire) for twenty years, and everyone who lived in SuperAsia (all the Asian countries became one) died off. When the ozone disappeared they all lived in a virtual reality pod. Every person was issued a "pillow partner," a life-size pillow that they spent their time with and attempted to sexually mate with. Due to the fact that everyone was fucking a pillow, Asians are now extinct.

For the last thirty years, after decades of drought and financial resource mismanagement, California was physically severed from the United States with giant drills and then pushed off into the ocean. In order to settle its massive debts, California was purchased by Scientologists, who now live on this island in the middle of the ocean. As a sovereign nation they are ruled by Tom Cruise, who obviously was once known as a prolific actor but now (thanks to technology that allows rich white people to live forever) is their reigning Kingdor.

The Scientologists bred every kind of animal together to create a superspecies, and Kingdor Cruise rides around on an ostrich with the head of a lion, which is pretty awesome. The garbage situation across the world has become unmanageable. Most cities in the United States are covered in those coffee cup pods that everyone used to love, which were completely hazardous and could never be destroyed but nobody fucking cared because one-touch, single-serve coffee was awesome. There are entire cities made from these little plastic cups. People live in actual houses made from hazelnut mocha pods.

In 2080, music is made solely on computers and would probably sound something akin to machines grinding to you, with beeps and boops and sometimes laser noises and the occasional human scream. Every person now has their own television network, broadcasting live twenty-four hours a day seven days a week, except that nobody is consuming any of it because everybody is so busy broadcasting their own meals and workouts.

Oh, I almost forgot, for many years being straight has been considered out of vogue and even offensive, and many heteros kept their sexuality closeted for fear of violence. In recent years those feelings have eased a bit, and it is now safe for a man and a woman to openly procreate.

I know the future probably doesn't sound that great, but despite all of that, I have good news to report. *No—great news.* With all the cross-breeding that has occurred over the last hundred years, there is no longer any single identifiable race in the continental United States. Black, Caucasian, Hispanic, Asian, Native American—they have all blended into one. What this means is that everyone's skin is a wonderful caramel hue, and all eye color variations blended together to become one magical green color that is honestly just so gorgeous. Imagine everyone looking like Rashida Jones. No really, close your eyes and imagine everybody being that fuckable. That is what is happening today. I remember years ago when not everyone was perfectly tan and people had brown eyes, and I can't even imagine how we had sex with one another. It's so horrible to imagine. Everyone now is exotic and has freckles, but like only a couple so it's cute, not like a weird amount. I had surgery in 2047 to look more like everyone else, and I look fucking great. Like amazing.

So the world is a garbage-covered mess filled with narcissistic freaks and we have no natural resources and people have forgotten how to experience most basic human emotions and nobody has hands so our every need is handled by machines, *but everyone has green eyes and is ridiculously good-looking.*

Is it really that bad? Definitely not. You should actually be looking forward to it. Good luck with hornet attack of 2066, and the whole Clooney as president debacle.

—Fat Jew

P.S. We cured cancer and AIDS and ugliness and it's super easy. I'll put it in another letter for my next book. But for this one I thought it would be best to tell you about fucked-up shit and how hot everyone looks.

After I read this letter I wrote from the future, I had my friend make a rendering of a house made of K-cup coffee trash. So...we're all basically fucked.

# MY BROTHER
# THE HERO

he fact that I share DNA with my brother, Avi, is one of the wondrous mysteries of the universe. We couldn't be more opposite—we're like black and white, sweet and savory, Kim Cattrall as Samantha on *Sex and the City* and Kim Cattrall in real life. In fact, the differences between me and my younger brother are straight out of a movie. And that movie exists and it is called *Twins*. You're going to be shocked, but I'm the Danny DeVito character. We split the gene pool traits directly down the middle, and we each got everything that the other one doesn't have. I got the incredible personality and the amazing sense of humor; he got the work ethic and a *tiny* head (look at it) and a *huge* penis. We couldn't be more different. Also, does Avi have a tiny head? Or are his muscles just sooooooooo big that he looks like he has a pinhead?

When we were kids, we had a pet turtle named Bruce. I liked

Bruce as much as anyone else, but since eleven-year-old me turned into the professional weirdo I am today, you can imagine that I was also into doing messed up stuff to him. I would draw dicks on his shell with whiteout, put Alka-Seltzer in his drinking water to see if it would make him explode—that type of shit. My brother would pretend to love these antics, often cheering me on in an effort to seem fun and irreverent. But secretly, as I later found out, he would clean Bruce's shell with a nontoxic solvent he had made from vinegar and water, and would often read books to him. My brother understood that he was part of something larger, a single grain of sand on an infinite beach of time. I just wanted to draw dicks on turtles. To this day, we are still in these exact same roles, my brother pretending to enjoy my antics while secretly cleaning up the mess.

Avi's an amateur bodybuilder who looks like a professional bodybuilder who does medical records structural analysis for the federal government. I think that's what he told me. He might be a spy. Regardless, he is a serious grown man with a mortgage and military security clearance, who drinks only Scotch aged in charred barrels. I guess in his scene he might be considered progressive, but trust me he's *not*, and that's why he's beautiful and special.

Although he is younger than I, he got married a few years ago, and due to familial obligation, I was his best man. As his best man, it was my responsibility (in addition to some other bullshit) to plan his bachelor party. The guys in the wedding party besides me were his three best friends: all normal white guys with normal bodies who do fantastically normal white guy stuff in their free time and have normal white people jobs. Sam is a middle school English teacher and lacrosse coach, Jake is also a middle school English teacher, and Jonathan (never John) is a podiatrist. *So normal.* Which coincidentally, I think, is why they looked to me to make my brother's bachelor party the wildest, stupidest, most hectic and "Fat Jew crazy" night of their lives.

The expectation was that my involvement would suddenly make everything more amazing. They loved my antics on the Internet and thought I was going to plan them a night that was going to be suuuuuper fun and funny and ridiculous. They wanted this party to be *The Hangover*, to wake up with no pants on with a live falcon perched on the couch next to them and be like *What happened???? Last night was nuts!!!!* So I gave them the carnival of sins they wanted.

We started the evening with dinner at Peter Luger Steak House in Brooklyn. If you've never been there, you should know that it's the type of place where there's essentially nothing to order but steak, steak for two, steak for three, and so on. We got steak, several orders of their bacon appetizer, which is thick-as-fuck bacon on a plate (I affectionately refer to it as Steak-con), and a lot of vodkas. Many, many, vodkas. All of the vodkas. Our seventy-year-old waiter, Tony, who coincidentally was vegan, took to us and kept our table flush with shots of vodka. He refused to bring us water, even when we asked him to. He thought it was funny. Tony had a great sense of humor. I think of him often.

By the time we'd literally licked our plates clean, we were all drunk. I gauge my after-dinner drunkenness by the amount of urine I'm able to get in the actual toilet bowl—after steaks, bacon, and vodka, I was able to get about half of it in. I was ready to start the night.

"Let's fucking go, you beautiful baby bitches," I commanded when I came back to the table. We got in a white Escalade that I'd generously chartered for the night and we were off to our next destination: an underground, traveling strip club called Saint Venus. It was about eleven p.m.

Saint Venus was my way of introducing the guys to the *true* energy of the night. The place isn't your average strip club, as in you can get away with sucking on a stripper's nipples or putting your finger in a butthole or two without being asked to leave. And the girls kind of look like normal girls, not as stripper-y as usual. But it's also not such an extreme environment that it might've scared these normal bros away from the rest of the night.

"This is the foreplay section of the night to come," I told them in the Escalade on the way.

"Can we all promise that no pictures will be taken of this night? Please?" an overly paranoid Sam asked the group.

"No pictures," I assured him. I remember glancing at my brother in the front seat of the SUV. He was smiling, and that warmed my cold heart for a fleeting moment. I was doing good by him, so far.

Tonight's location for Saint Venus was across the Williamsburg Bridge in the basement of an office building in lower Manhattan. I love these traveling smut bars. It's one of my favorite things about NYC. It moves around, similar to a circus (of vaginas), and it's normally located in an empty office or a hotel suite. It costs fifty bucks for entry, but that includes a drink and free pasta, which I know sounds gross, but the fusilli with garden vegetables is actually delightful. The vibe of Saint Venus is not scary, but it's not cute. Lots of smoke machines.

When we walked in, I could tell by the looks on the guys' faces that this was *new* to them. Brand fucking new. They looked like kids in a candy store, except for the fact that the candy was actually average-to-hot strippers. Yeah, the guys were in heaven.

"These are the hottest strippers I've ever seen."

"Yeah. They are really hot. Why are they so hot?"

"They're hot because we're in an insurance office on Jay Street. There is something inherently unsexy about strip clubs, and when you take that element away, you realize that it's all about tits and ass."

We ordered some shots and got situated at a corner table. My brother refused to get a lap dance because of his pending nuptials, but as the rest of us received the ones that I'd organized ahead of time (because I'm a loving brother), I glanced over at him and I saw him yawn.

"I'm sorry, Megan," I said to the girl on my lap. Her name probably wasn't Megan, but to me it definitely was. "I'm gonna have to cancel this dance right now." I softly nudged her off, stood up, and walked over to my brother's chair.

"We're leaving."

"What. Why?" He looked disappointed. He also looked drunk as *fuck*.

"Because you just yawned and that's unacceptable. There is no yawning on my watch."

"I literally got up at five forty-five this morning to work out..."

"Nope. Don't care. I don't want to hear about this shit. We are taking care of this sleepy adult thing you have going on right now."

My reputation as a maniac was not going to be called into question by this night not being fucking awesome. We had to take things to the next level.

Ten minutes later, the five of us were standing in the lobby of the building waiting for my coke dealer, René. He's black and French, not the white woman you just pictured, you racist asshole.

"I haven't really done some cocaine since like, uhh, college, Josh. I don't fucking know, man. Do not think it's a good idea for me to be like, uhh, doing cocaine when I have to wake up for the kids' school tomorrow, my man," Jake slurred.

"First of all," I said to him, "tomorrow is Sunday, so fuck your kids. Wait, that sounded weird. Your kids are fine. I saw them on Instagram. They're really cute. Second, cocaine is never a bad idea. Especially when you're in an office building in Koreatown."

René walked in. He'd been my dealer, on and off, for years. He was a good guy with a cleft lip and who wore permanently clean black Timberlands, even in the summer. He would also wear numerous wristwatches at once, nice ones with diamonds, sometimes four or even six on each wrist. It was his thing. Plus, his cocaine was good. So good, in fact, that I'll probably never achieve an erection again.

"How much do you want?" René asked. He was such a French hunk.

"I'll take an eight ball."

The transaction was quick and easy. I bought way too much, about a gram and a half for each of us, but at the time it felt like not nearly enough.

Without "naming names," some of us did key bumps of coke there in the lobby in front of probably six surveillance cameras that were most definitely (maybe) not plugged into any power source, and we were on our way. Avi did not partake, but I didn't want to make a big deal out of it. The excitement of scoring drugs had woken him up a lot, and that was my primary objective. Also, his friends were starting to have a really good time, and that seemed to make Avi super happy. That's just the kind of A+ guy he is.

I'm not sure any of these guys had a serious night out before, and by *I'm not sure* I mean completely sure, because these dudes were immediately mangled. We stopped in at a few scummy bars in Midtown and got more hammered, then Jonathan farted shit into his underpants, so we had to send him home in a car service.

"I think I need to be done," Avi said to me, slumped on a bar stool in the back of the neon-lit bar where the four of us were drinking Japanese beers and exchanging stories about summer camp. I shook my head slowly. In that moment, I was his disappointed mom who just wanted her son to grow some fucking nuts and rally. Luckily, he did. :)

"*Dog fighting!!!!!*" I screamed very loudly right into his face.

I brought them to a little weekly Dominican dog-fighting get-together on the Lower East Side that I knew was en route to our final destination. I really thought these guys would appreciate the experience.

I was wrong.

"This is fucked up," Sam announced to the group of us, the whitest people in the room, raising his voice to be heard over the roar of a hundred Dominicans waving money around and screaming at top volume. Great, Sam. Way to be a team player.

"It's fiiiiine," I assured them. "You guys all do your little fantasy football or baseball or whatever, right? Just think of it like that. Bet on the dogs with the least scars and make a few bucks."

"I'm ashamed to be here," Sam kept on saying.

"You'll want the extra cash at the next stop, trust me."

They grew some balls and bet on a few fights. They were totally right, btw—dog fighting is actually disgusting and depressing— but we tried to have fun. Seeing it through their eyes made me realize the error of my ways. They actually ruined dog fighting for me forever.

"Okay, Okay," I finally said after an hour of dogs barking, cash flying, and scary men screaming around them.

"I know everyone is tired and it's three in the morning. But I love you, Avi, and I think we *actually* need to hang out right now." That very easily might've been the first time I'd ever said that to him. In that moment he looked so loveable and brother-y.

Jake winked at me, which was odd, but I guess he felt the energy of our bro-ment, too. Bro-ment?

Needless to say, I got the men to agree to come along to the last and most important scheduled event of the bachelor party: an illegal, all-tranny sex circus in a warehouse in deep Brooklyn. Not *fun, cute, white people having brunch* Brooklyn. Not even *currently undergoing gentrification semi-scary* Brooklyn. We're talking about the part of Brooklyn where everyone is Eastern European and has a unibrow. I let them know that this place was cool and trustworthy, and they were fucked up enough to believe me.

My brother was extremely drunk, and his friends were also wrecked. In fact, they had no idea that the chicks giving them very private, very sensual lap dances were actually transgendered. They must have thought this was like the first illegal strip club, from earlier. It was all a bit of a blur, but one highlight for sure was when Avi vomited in the middle of the makeshift dance floor, narrowly missing my bare chest. I'd been shirtless since the last Korean bar we stopped into.

Instead of cleaning up his mess, my brother relocated to a dark and dingy corner of the club, found his balance, and puked some more. He rallied like a pro, and I loved him for it.

We stayed at the spot in Brooklyn for about an hour before realizing that it wasn't us that smelled like shit—it was the place. Also, Jake and Sam ended up feeling the semi-erect penises on the strippers that were giving them their respective lap dances. They *really* couldn't deal with that. We needed to stop. The sun was up, we were hungry again somehow, and it was simply *that time of the night/morning.* Sam and Jake went home, and my brother and I went to our favorite childhood diner. Sitting across from Avi, back in Manhattan, it struck me that we might not be as different as I always thought.

"This was mad fun," I said to Avi.

"Pshhhhhhh it's erben," he responded, in what sounded like complete and utter nonsense.

"Right, exactly."

"En dow bay. En dow bay, Josh."

Most people would have been frustrated by the fact they couldn't understand their brother, but to me this was a special moment. It was the first time in his life that he wasn't making sense. It was freeing for him and for me. By not understanding him, I finally understood him.

Weeks later, at the wedding, Sam, Jake, and Jonathan were acting strange. I was even semi-excited to see them and to remind Jonathan about that time a few weeks back when he shit in his seafoam-green Polo pants and we all laughed. But the guys were

acting like we didn't even know each other, like we hadn't shared the best night of their lives together. Nobody wanted to talk about it, no one was reminiscing with me, and all of their wives were looking at me like I was the fucking devil. I felt snubbed, embarrassed, and alone on my brother's big day.

I felt shitty. Had I gone too far? Maybe I went too far. Maybe I screwed up and took it to places I never should have. Goddammit. He is my brother, after all, not some douchebag boyfriend of an old camp friend that I'm just trying to fuck with 'cause it's his first night in NYC or whatever.

At the drinking part of the wedding, I pulled my brother and the guys aside.

"Look, I get it. I took it to the edge with the dog fighting and the coke and the trannies and I'm sorry."

They looked at me blankly.

"Okay. Wow, you're just gonna do me like that. All right." I threw my hands up and started to walk away, managing to grab a shrimp off a platter as I turned around.

"Josh," Avi said in a hushed voice. "The night was genius."

"Yeah." "Yes." "I was reborn that night," echoed the rest of the guys.

"I thought you were mad because I like disrespected your marriage or some shit," I said.

"Not at all," Avi assured me.

"Josh, that was the singular best night of my life. It's just my wife got mad that I came home at eight that morning smelling like booze and lube."

"I have no idea. But we told all of our wives that it was kind of boring, so they didn't ask too many questions."

I then remembered that, unlike me, a person who talks about a dog fighting and transvestite rave night at any and every opportunity, these guys have real jobs and real lives, and they have to downplay the epicness of the night as not to have to divulge details that could get them into trouble. I was so happy that I delivered the "Fat Jew" night that they wanted.

"Jonathan, remember how you got so drunk that you shit in your khakis?"

"Honestly...*I don't!*"

We all began to laugh, and toasted our glasses. I was happy.

# 17.

# SHARON STONE, AN OSTRICH, AND AN OCEAN OF ROSÉ

nfluencer (n.): An individual who is well connected, has impact and an active mind, and is a trendsetter who can significantly shape the customer's purchasing decision but may never be accountable for it.

In layman's terms it means that if you have a large social following either online or in real life, you can get paid money to talk about stuff. I'm an *influencer*. Companies pay me to put their product on Facebook/Instagram/Twitter and pretend that I actually use it, so that the teens who follow me will buy said product.

The much more awesome component is when I get sent to events, sponsored by a brand, to do *absolutely nothing*. All I have to do is stand around in some sort of ridiculous outfit that I would normally wear to a party (thong, Rollerblades, or wetsuit) and just look cool. In turn, the brand looks cool because I'm hanging out at their party. It's an easy gig, but it comes fraught with moments of deep, deep self-hatred. But that's every job, right? Overall, I feel incredibly blessed to be able to call it my life while some people are slaving away doing lame stuff, like being teachers and doctors.

A few months ago, Stella Artois called and asked me if I would fly to France to attend a bunch of parties that they were hosting at the Cannes Film Festival. If you don't know, the Cannes Film Festival is a yearly celebration of the newest films spanning all genres from around the globe. It's the most celebrated and famous film festival in the world. It dates back to the 1940s and is steeped in tradition. I like to think of it as the European Academy Awards, but in reality the Oscars are just our fake Birkin bag knockoff of Cannes.

It's the second largest media event in the world behind only the Olympics. Two thousand films are screened over the course of twelve days to colossal fanfare. Cannes is also famed for showcasing emerging directors, where future Quentin Tarantinos and George Lucases gain their first large-scale recognition and launch their wildly successful careers. The festivities culminate with one film being awarded the Palme d'Or, honoring the festival's greatest cinematic achievement, an award that is unparalleled in its prestige within the world of film. LOLOLOLOLOLOLOL. *You guys, I'm just kidding.* Imagine if I actually gave a shit about the "rich tradition" of Cannes? Can you imagine? I do not.

But I did go, and honestly if Stella Artois ever wants to pay for you to go as well, say yes, because it's a playground for uber-rich European morons with natural tans so deep that they can be achieved only by riding horseback every day on a beach. At Cannes, you're surrounded by guys from Monaco drinking rosé at eight o'clock in the morning, who will metaphorically (and, as I found out one night, also literally) dump money into the fucking ocean. People wear tuxedos *at all times*, use croissants as loofahs, and wipe their tanned butts and bleached buttholes with fresh truffles.

So, I'm sent there to hang out at some parties Stella Artois is throwing to celebrate all this nonsense. They weren't paying me much, but I didn't care because it was going to be such an ultimate shitshow that I accepted the job with a resounding "*Yasss*," packed my thong and tuxedo, and flew to France. A lot of good things happened over the course of five days, but only one event really mattered, so I figured I'd share with you because it's awesome, and your life will be 0.001 percent better after reading it. Yes, I'm a giver.

One night I was at a Stella-sponsored party and some rich Saudi dudes noticed me. They were intimidating and beautiful and looked rich as *mother*fuck. I knew they were kind of obsessed with me because the first thing they said to me, in their thick, delicious accent was: "Dude, Fat Mr. Jew, we are kind of obsessed with you, buddy."

"What?" I replied, taken aback.

"We know you from the Internet, you fuckin' madman," one of them said with a huge smile. I wasn't dreaming. These Saudis were actual fans.

"Okay. Well, thanks, dudes. It's nice to meet you guys. Thanks for saying hi—"

"You need come with us tonight and join the entourage, as you say," said the first guy.

"Join the entourage?"

"Yes, what do you think I fucking said, you fat fuck?" he said, causing the entire group to erupt in howling laughter. I was in.

A few hours later I found myself at a party on a yacht belonging to one of them (boat soirées are extremely common at Cannes), and this is exactly what happened: Sharon Stone was possibly coked up and talking to me and some "movie producers" from Eastern Europe about her experience filming the 1992 classic film *Basic Instinct*.

I don't know if she was high. I didn't see her do drugs, but I know what it looks like when people are on drugs. Let's all be adults about this, oka? (It should be noted that I don't really know what Sharon Stone is like when she is not high, but it would be different than the way she was acting on the yacht that day.) This is how the conversation went:

**SHARON:**

Ask me who my inspiration was for my character in the film.

**EASTERN EUROPEAN "MOVIE PRODUCER":**

Please tell us, Sharon.

**SHARON:**

Magic Johnson. (*Smokes an entire cigarette in one single drag.*) The way he played the game of basketball, that's how I act. (*Now screaming*) I *want to dazzle!* Have you ever seen him throw a no-look pass? That's how I am with the camera. I'm looking somewhere else, and then all of a sudden *bam!* I'm throwing the energy to you.

**EASTERN EUROPEAN "MOVIE PRODUCERS":**

Yes, yes, that makes total sense. I love that.

**ME:**

*What?* [I should mention that I said this internally. Outwardly, I nodded like everyone else.]

Then things turned up to another level of awesome. One of the Saudi dudes from earlier who had identified himself as Kevin tapped me on the shoulder and motioned for me to follow. We headed into the lower level of the yacht, and suddenly stopped at a random door. "I wanted you to see this, Mr. Jewish."

I assumed that the room would be filled with gold bullion and prostitutes, or possibly a woman with two vaginas, but it turned out to be even weirder. The room was completely empty, save for a stereo that was softly playing "Party Rock" by LMFAO and an ostrich. Yes, a single, glorious ostrich. I'd never seen one in

person before. It was very big. And very much an
alien from space. I couldn't take my eyes off of
the thing.

"Do not enter the room," Kevin whispered.

"Why?" I asked, also whispering.

"This is Bradley Cooper, and he does not like to
be touched or disturbed."

I was coked up, and this was exploding my mind to shreds.
The ostrich was just walking around the room, listening to bad
Top 40 music, just chilling. *OK OK OK, let's review the facts: I'm in
the south of France wearing a tuxedo and I'm on a yacht with some Saudi
Arabians who are richer than God, and they have an ostrich in a room for
absolutely no fucking reason, and they named it Bradley Cooper because
they love the actor Bradley Cooper.*

As Bradley and I stared deep into each other's eyes, something
profound occurred to me: He, like me, is an exotic bird who gets
taken around the world and put into lavish and bizarre situations
just because of how awesome he is. The Saudis love Bradley
because he is colorful, a little bit scary, and makes for a great
story. Now I know what you might be thinking: "Fat Jew, you
don't want to be anyone's pet. Never let people treat you like an
animal." And my response to that would be that you are correct.
I, of course, would never want to be objectified and treated like
some kind of dancing clown. I'm a human man and an artist who
demands respect. *Unlesssssss*...there's unlimited rosé and Sharon
Stone is there talking about her acting career, and I'm on a yacht
in France, and there's lots of free drugs, and everyone is wearing

a tuxedo, and I'm surrounded by Saudis who are billionaires, in which case, I'll basically do *whatever*.

I realize, after having written so many stories for this book, that each chapter needs to have a beginning, middle, and end. But you know what? Fuck that. I do whatever I want. *I'm a grownup.* You cannot do any better than ending your story with a cathartic, watershed moment with an ostrich named Bradley Cooper. You just can't. So I'm ending this chapter right here. Fuck you, Mrs. Geary, my eleventh-grade AP English teacher, and *fuck you* to all the h8ers!!!!

18.

# MY GROUPIES
# NEED JESUS

'm basically a Z-list celebrity. Which in this day and age means that I'm famous for no real reason, yet somehow, people still pay attention to me and what I do. It also means that I have *psychotic groupies*. Obviously, I'm not a member of Guns N' Roses in 1990, or David Hasselhoff in Germany. We're not talking about leggy blondes grabbing at me, trying to rip my dick off so they can bronze it and make a necklace to wear.

Think more fours and fives who have giant lady hands, hate their dads, and are from gross cities like Fresno and Wichita. Frankly, I'm totally fine with that. You know why? Because I'm sure the woman who'd let Jude Law get inside of her pink satin seashell is much hotter in every physical sense than the girls who want to fuck me, but my groupies have something that Jude Law's groupies don't have. They're all *insane*.

And, fortunately for me, *crazy* is what gets me sexually aroused. I've had fans let me do all types of stuff to them. One time I was at a Kid Rock concert in Detroit and two overweight Midwestern gals who think my Instagram is hilarious and "sooooo us" (their words, verbatim) fought each other in the front seat of a pickup truck in order to get to hang out with me for the entire concert. I initially suggested it as a joke, but they were *down*. Imagine two big girls fighting each other in a 3×3-foot space. It was scary and exhilarating and, honestly, more entertaining than Kid Rock's performance.

My hard-core female fans need round-the-clock therapy. They are emotionally unstable and battling serious demons. I feel bad for them, but at the same time I've looked at so much horrible imagery on the Internet that I killed my own sex drive, and the only way I can get sexually aroused these days is feeding off the insanity of those women who religiously follow my goings-on. The crazier the better. The wilder the scenario, the more I love it. Nothing is ever too far for me.

Some examples:

### LAUREN

Height: 5 foot 4    Weight: 130 pounds    Hair: Brown

Issue: Historically accurate pervert

Lauren was definitely psychotic, but unlike some of the maniacs I've fornicated with, she was incredibly smart. She went to graduate school at Stanford, where she majored in something incredibly specific that has zero application in the real world, like seventeenth-century women's instruments. We met on the Internet (I know, you're shocked) back in the Myspace days, and it turned out that she lived close by. She was a total five. There was nothing remarkable about her whatsoever. She looked like a baked potato, no toppings, with legs.

My expectation was that her seemingly normal exterior was housing a myriad of emotional problems, and that she would probably be the weirdest girl I've ever had sex with. *Nope.* We began banging regularly, and as they always do with me, things got boring fast. But this time, it wasn't just my insatiable thirst for an awesome sexual encounter story; it was also that she was not into *anything* cool. She wasn't into butt eating or bruising or dressing me like a baby and breastfeeding me, and I started thinking that maybe she just wasn't a weirdo. Again, *nope.* One night, while texting, I jokingly suggested that we have an OJ trial fantasy and I took a screenshot of her response:

---

**MESSAGE**
Today 22/07/2007 3:56 PM

JOSH  You know what would be amazing?

JOSH  If we did an OJ Simpson Trial Fantasy

LAUREN  That is such a weird idea. Who is who?

JOSH  I'm OJ, and you're Judge Lance Ito with boobs

LAUREN LOL

---

She didn't actually LOL in real life. I just knew it. She wanted no part of my OJ sex fantasy.

A week later we made plans for sex, but it was going to be my last time seeing her, because she was just too...*normal.* She had a good job and was close with her father and drank only wine with dinner and made good life choices and it was making me fucking sick. I was happy that she was doing so well, but it doesn't give me boners. I want someone spiraling. When I arrived at her house for some mediocre sex and a pleasant goodbye forever, my mind was melted. Lauren had set up her apartment to look like a courtroom, complete with juror seats, a makeshift judge's bench with a gavel on it, and a wooden chair with fencing around it serving as the stand in a courtroom. Lauren was wearing a judge's robe, a black comb-over wig, and a fucking Fu Manchu mustache. I didn't take a photo, but if you're too young to remember, this is Judge Lance Ito (also, I want to have sex with you, too).

She had a navy suit for me with a patterned tie that, upon a Google search, I found to be strikingly similar to the outfit that OJ frequently wore during his trial. She even had a leather glove that didn't fit my hand. *The accuracy was incredible.* The sex was a little over the top, and at one point she jammed a finger directly into my butthole.

"No!" I yelped, surprised and not that into ass play.

"*Objection overruled!*" she bellowed out, followed by a deep laugh.

I was scared, but also so very turned on.

Over the next few weeks, we did more historical-themed fuck sessions—the Civil War, the shining, JonBenét Ramsey, spring break Daytona Beach 1992—and each one was handled with the same level of focus and attention to detail. Somehow she managed to obtain a musket for the Civil War fantasy! A musket! It turned out that Lauren actually *was* a psychotic sexual deviant—I just had to dig deep, and it turned out to be historical accuracy that made her a legendary psychotic groupie.

## NINA

Height: 5 foot 1    Weight: 100 pounds, maybe    Hair: Black

Issue: Stalking

Stalking is scary. It's intense, it's creepy, it's really dark, *but*...it can also be super fun and a total turn-on if done the right way. Nina was my prototype groupie: She loved cocaine, had serious self-esteem issues, and was a chuckle fucker. Yes, a chuckle fucker. Girls who fuck funny guys. It's hard to spot a chuckle fucker. Sometimes they are overweight girls who try to do stand-up comedy, so it makes total sense, and sometimes it's a blonde publicist with a terrible attitude who is a nine and just happens to love fucking fat guys who make the LOLs. They're sometimes hard to spot. Nina and I met on Facebook. We had some mutual friends in common, and she seemed like she wanted my mangled little rock shrimp penis inside of her. We met at a nightclub blah-blah-blah and ended up at her dumpy one-bedroom in Tribeca. She was standard run-of-the-mill wild at first, like she was game to lick my taint (sorry, Mom; sorry, everyone) and would aggressively swing her hair around while on top of me during sex. It was forced. I lost interest after a month and stopped responding to her text messages, which upset her greatly. A lot of four thirty a.m. texts like this started coming my way:

"You're a dick. Bye forever. Dick."

It wasn't even that fun or psycho, more "angry white girl drunk on white wine."

But the more I let her twist in the wind, the more wild she got. The less I did, the more she became a monster. I started getting four thirty a.m. texts like this:

"I'm going to rip your dick off and stab you to death with it"

*Yes. Now we're talking.*

Then she started stalking me.

She was really good at it too, like actually *extremely* talented. She should probably work for a private government agency. She would pop up in the strangest places, like sitting a few rows in front of me at the DMV, or wearing a trench coat with a hat at a diner where I was eating, peering over the menu. Movie-type shit. A company wanted to hire me to shoot a funny Internet video, and

when I walked into the first meeting to meet their team, she was on it—and pretended not to know me. I came outside my house one day, and she was tanning on a lawn chair in a parking spot with a meter that she was feeding quarters. Such a good look!

The stalking led to renewed interest on my part, and we continued seeing each other until she had some sort of mental breakdown and went back to Ohio. I miss her every day.

•

But there was one really magical girl. A true psycho. The one who will always hold the most special place in my heart.

## LINDSAY

Height: 5 foot 4    Weight: 120 pounds    Hair: Dirty blonde
Issue: Sooo many

Lindsay was from Sacramento, which is disgusting, but she had everything else that I ever wanted in a groupie: She was Jewish, she had mediocre work done so her boobs were rock solid (I love bad plastic surgery), she had a tattoo on her rib cage that said "Regret Nothing," and most of all, she was a *legendary* mess.

Sidenote

I don't throw the word *legendary* around much anymore because it got ruined by frat bros who insisted on referring to every single night where they drank a lot of booze and date raped a girl as "legendary," but Lindsay from Sacramento really deserves it. Partially because she was diagnosed bipolar and decided to substitute her prescribed medication with cocaine, but also because she was also a very gifted painter, and although that kind of talent can most certainly be used for productive and good things, in this case it was channeled into craziness.

I met Lindsay through social media, when I tweeted out "hey can a girl on here shave their pubic hair and mail it to me so I can smoke it in a joint?" and she immediately responded. It was the fastest response time ever. As in Chinese food delivery on Christmas Day fast. She agreed to do it, and five days later I received an envelope from California containing a handful of pubes, and I proceeded to smoke them out of a bong and put video footage of it up on YouTube. An incredibly toxic/beautiful relationship was born.

**Sidenote**

Never smoke women's pubic hairs. Not to be funny, not to be cool, not ever. They smell insane once you light them on fire, and will make you feel like you are going to vomit all over yourself.

From there, things took off. We messaged back and forth about various things, most of them consisting of innuendos about making sex with each other. It was just a game. She told me she was nineteen years old and used to be Goth, but dropped that look and became a standard party animal. Eventually the conversation moved over to text messaging.

But then, one Tuesday as I sat at my computer with my glass of morning rosé, I got a picture message from her that indicated to me that this relationship was about to take a turn for the worse or maybe the best—or maybe it would be both. This was it:

I had to meet her.

Lindsay flew to New York and stayed in some shitty midtown hotel for the first few nights because I wasn't just going to let her into my home without first vetting her actual level of insanity. I wanted to meet her first, take her out to a meal, and get to know her craziness IRL. I also needed to make sure she wasn't a Serbian man catfishing me.

I met Lindsay at an Italian restaurant with reasonably priced entrées, and we got to know each other. She was worse looking in person because, you know, the Internet, but she was surprisingly well spoken and knew how to use a fork and knife properly. We spent the meal making some light conversation, but for the most part, she seemed extremely shy and understated. Until we got back to her hotel.

"I'm gonna use the bathroom," I said as we entered the room.

"Sure. You're going to fuck me, but first, I'm gonna take a bath, and I was hoping you could hold your pee for a sec and let me get situated in the tub first."

"That's awesome. But, why do I have wait? I really have to pee, bad."

"Great, that's even better. Just hold on. Give me two minutes," Lindsay said as she ripped off her top, revealing those amazing sweater puppets I'd seen in the photo. She then ran into the bathroom and turned on the bath.

"Okay. I'm ready," she called out not a minute later.

When I entered the tiny hotel bathroom I found Lindsay in the tub smiling.

"Hey, I'm gonna pee now," I said.

"Pee on my feet."

"Really?"

"Please. Pretty please."

I really had no choice. It was surprisingly awesome and very sexually satisfying to degrade her in this way. What a weirdo.

Over the next three days, we got pretty deviant. Got into classic stuff like anal, screaming into her vagina at top volume, Lindsay filling her mouth with horseradish and then giving me fellatio, cock rings, milk play, gagging, taco time (Google these if you don't know about them). It was 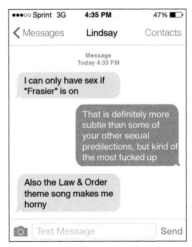 great. However, after she left I began to notice some red flags that indicated she wasn't your average psycho groupie.

●●●○○ Sprint 3G   4:23 PM   47% ▭

‹ Messages   **Lindsay**   Contacts

Message
Today 4:23 PM

You know what one of my main turn ons is?

Do tell

Abortions

📷 Text Message   Send

●●●○○ Sprint 3G   4:35 PM   47% ▭

‹ Messages   **Lindsay**   Contacts

Message
Today 4:33 PM

I can only have sex if "Frasier" is on

That is definitely more subtle than some of your other sexual predilections, but kind of the most fucked up

Also the Law & Order theme song makes me horny

📷 Text Message   Send

Listen, I am definitely into my share of creepy sexual activities, so who am I to judge? I thought she was just trying to impress me by being extreme, so I really didn't pay it much mind. Over the next few months we chatted from time to time. We sent each other pics of our genitalia and other fun things. We were keeping things light, and she seemed to be maintaining her cool.

Then...I went to San Francisco for a video shoot, and I arranged to meet up with her. Lindsay lived in a mediocre apartment upstairs from a Yankee Candle company store, which, as you can imagine, smelled very intense. One candle can make your home smell inviting and lovely, but all of them mixed together smells very, very gross. I could taste it in my mouth.

"Hey. Nice place," I said.

I entered the apartment, and everything was so normal for a twenty-two-year-old. Not at all what I expected: That poster of a soldier kissing a girl in Paris on the wall. Think Ikea, but like nice Ikea. Classy coffee table books. A bowl sitting on a little kitchen table filled with pears. A relatively new flat screen TV. Pictures of Linsday with her whole family looking sooooo happy on a beach. A badass Johnny Cash poster that was purchased at an Urban Outfitters.

Maybe she wasn't as crazy as I thought she was.

"I'm so glad you came out to see me. I really missed you." Lindsay was smiling.

But then we walked into her bedroom.

It was fucking mental. Like really fucking mental. Apparently Lindsay's obsession had spiraled since our time spent in New

York, and now her bedroom was *filled* with paintings of me and of us together, of me and her on horseback galloping through outer space, me ejaculating a rainbow, and one of me, her, and Morgan Freeman having dinner and laughing together. But the one that really fucked me up was massive and hanging directly over her bed.

It was me, as Jesus, nailed to the cross. My body was blood, but instead of actual nails going through my hands and feet, she'd painted little Lindsays that were pinning me to the cross. It was really freaky. It was definitely terrifying, but you have to remember that I really thrive on this type of stuff. Basically it became immediately apparent that she was not well, and I was probably actually in physical danger, but my ego is so big that it was *nice* to see all the paintings. I embraced that shit. She was overjoyed that I didn't immediately leave. Although I definitely should have. I should have run out, gotten in my Chevy Malibu rental, and driven into the smoggy California sunset. But I stayed and spent the night. A night that can never been unlived.

After seeing her shrine I decided I could take the sexual creativity to the next level, the level that makes for stories I could tell at dinner parties for years to come.

"I want to put you in the dryer," I said.

"Sure," she replied, without even skipping a beat.

Lindsay was about five foot four and 120 pounds, so it was totally doable. Now I know you might see that as potentially dangerous, and you should know that you are completely right. But I love a good story and am a habitual line crosser, and this girl was willing to do anything I asked, so I had to do it. We had left the realm of sexual deviancy and went into straight-up sexual *danger*.

"Do you have a washer/dryer?"

"Do you have laundry you want done?" she asked creepily.

"Yes. But first, I want you to get inside the dryer. It's  a fantasy I've had forever," I said, which was funny because I had come up with the idea roughly five minutes earlier.

"So, I'm just gonna get naked and climb inside for you."

Her willingness to please me while in the face of such ridiculous and scary circumstances was a major turn-on. Sound the alarm. *Boner alert.*

I pressed the Start button, and immediately heard a horrific scream and a loud thump. I understood the thump to be her body making a rotation and falling from top to bottom, but did it really hurt that badly? I opened the door and she jumped out, holding her arm and running to the bathroom.

"Fuck fuck fuck I'm burned!" she screamed, and instantaneously my little Jewish erection disappeared.

"Okay, Okay, stay calm, maybe just run it under some water!" I shrieked.

She had indeed been badly burned, because what I didn't know was that when you push the start button on a dryer, flames shoot up behind a metal grate in the back of the machine. The reason most of us don't know this is because we don't look inside when the dryer starts, and most of us are not making naked girls get in there. The water was making the burn worse, and I had turned from Z-list celebrity sex god to neurotic Jewish mother in a matter of seconds.

"Wait, maybe we should put something on it!" I yelled while frantically scouring for what that item would be. I flung open the fridge and ripped open the vegetable drawer and grabbed the first thing I saw: a squash.

*"Hold this on your arm!"* I screamed while trying to hand it to her.

"Is that a...squash? You brought me a fucking squash??"

"It's like putting a steak on a black eye, it's cold. *I don't know.*"

She threw the squash at me, and it barely missed. Things were getting very Ike and Tina, and to be honest I was kind of getting sexually aroused again.

After twenty minutes of holding her arm under water, it was clear that we needed actual medical attention. We hopped in my shitty rental car and I drove her to the Sacramento General ER. As we sat there waiting to be seen, I looked at this girl clutching her arm and making weird noises while laying on my chest, and I realized something, something meaningful, something adult:

Maybe this was too far.

Sidenote

Listen up, men: If you're like me and regular sex just doesn't cut it, like you'd get more turned on by shaving off a girl's pubic hair and smoking it in a joint and then letting her speedbag your balls than just having normal sex, it's going to take some convincing. The average beautiful self-respecting woman is just not going to be into it. The way the world works is that if you're a sexual deviant and you want to convince a girl to do deviant and dark sexual stuff with you, it helps if you are one of three things: rich, hunky, or famous. I ate frozen burritos for all three meals today, so I'm definitely not rich, and I have a body like a snowman, so I'm certainly not hunky, but I am marginally famous. I'm gonna milk that for everything it's worth. Are you none of those three? Then go to www.thrinder.com (threesome Tinder). Every girl on there is fucking insane and will do whatever. (Disclaimer: if you are murdered, it's soooooo not my fault.) (I'll always continue to be attracted to this kind of insanity. It's just who I am.)

19.
CHILL ZONE #4

# HAIKU

Jason Biggs from *American Pie*

Isn't Jewish.

Really think about that.

## MUSIC

There's something we all need to admit.

We must stop lying to ourselves.

Deceiving ourselves.

Being disingenuous with one another.

The Doors suck. Bad.

## HOW BURY A BODY

? ? ? ? ? ? ? ? ? ?

1. Kill someone (or find a dead body?)

2. Wrap it in a bed sheet.

3. drag the body to your car.

4. Get DNA evidence all over your car.

5. Get seen by many people dragging the body to a field.

6. Dig a big whole and put the body in it.

7. Act nervous around everyone that you know .

8. Lie to your loved ones.

9. Lie to the police when they question you, poorly.

10. Look sweaty and tired because you can't sleep due to crippling guilt.

11. Get arrested for murder and spend the rest of your life in jail.

Last night after grandpas funeral, i started thinking about what if our dog Bruce died would daddy cry like he died at grandpas funeral. When dad cried today it made me feel really weird and I wondered if he is a man or no. I know boys and girls cry but why do old people cry because when he did it it looked like he was going to throw up like that time I first tried sushi. I asked mommy about it after the funeral when we were eating bagels and everyone was at our house talking about our cousin Phil who brought his roommate Ted to the service and now that wasn't right. I couldnt tell why it wasn't right or not but when i asked mommy she said yes, your dad is all man and smiled and winked at my aunt and then they both started laughing. I felt embarrassed and said grandpas dead and ran to my room and wanted to play sonic the hedgehog but i had lent the game out to Nick so i just sat in my room and made sounds like i was playing sonic. If dad cries again, i'm going to ask him if he is a boy or a girl. i'm not angry at him, i just need to know.

today in class i had to get up in front of everyone and make a speech on abraham lincoln and how he freed the slaves and i was really nervous. i asked my dad if i could rehearse with him the night before and he said after 60 minutes so i unplugged the TV and he looked at me for a while, and then he asked me if i thought he was an idiot and i said abraham lincoln was our president and he freed the slaves and then my dad got up and walked out of the room. so then i went and asked my mom but she was doing the exercise video where it looks like she's making sex with the air and she was sweating and making sounds like when you have to take a num ber two really badly. so i went to my room and started screaming my speech until my mommy and daddy both came to the door of my bedroom and watched me and they looked scared but i didn't stop my speech. well it doesn't matter anyway because when i gave my speech to my class the next day i farted in the middle of it but blamed it on the new kid toby who everyone thinks is retarded or something.

THIS COUPON IS GOOD FOR:

# THIS COUPON IS GOOD FOR:

A NUDE

THIS COUPON IS GOOD FOR:

*1 Ride to the Airport*

20.

# AVAILABLE FOR BAR MITZVAHS, QUINCEAÑERA'S & GRADUATIONS

ere's the deal: I'm the future. Not in like a Kanye "I'm actually from a time and place that hasn't happened yet," but more of a "what I do for work is really where things are heading" type of way. All the real adults who are reading this book may not want to accept it, but I'm telling you, it's the truth. And it occurs to me that I get paid to make appearances at bar mitzvahs and DJ quinceañeras, but what I really should be doing is giving keynote speeches at high school and college graduations. So if you're the dean at one of these types of educational institutions, you should know that I'm now accepting offers to speak at your school's graduation. You may not like how this sounds, but trust me, this is what the kids want. Also, I'm *nice* at public speaking. Let me give you a little sample of my shit:

*(I bust through a giant piece of white paper like at a high school football game. I'm wearing a cap and gown, while the band Rush plays live behind me.)*

To the graduating class of this year, congratulations. It's an honor to be here and a privilege to spend these, your final moments as students at this incredible institution, with you. You know, people ask me all the time what it is that I do for a living. Surely a great question, but strangely enough, I don't know exactly what I do. I know that I make videos and I post funny things online. I know people pay me to host events and to be at certain parties. But the truth about the jobs landscape at this moment in our country's history is that you don't have to do a traditional type of job anymore. In fact, I encourage you not to.

There used to only be about ten things that you could do for a living: doctor, lawyer, teacher, secretary, accountant, fireman, policeman—you get the picture. But forget that. We've moved beyond all of that. The traditional media will try their best to scare you into thinking that the job market is soft and that it's never been harder to get work. *But that is all lies!!!*

*(Bang fist on podium, take dramatic pause.)*

It's never been easier to get a job than right now. Every single tech company and app company employs people and gives them completely made-up titles. I know a guy who just got hired by the largest social media platform in the world—it begins with F and ends with *book*—and his job title is *Cryptocurrencies Czar*. I'm not even kidding. That is a real job at a real company whose stock is traded on the New York Stock Exchange.

So, you should ask yourself as you set out on this next phase of your life, What kind of job do I want to have? Instagrammer in Residence? Resident Tech Specialist? Snackable Content Mastermind? SVP of Digital Imaging and Hyper Local Activations? Just make up a job title and then go from there. You'll figure the rest out once you convince one of these companies to hire you. You're super smart. You are graduating from this place, so you're definitely not a complete dumb-dumb. Have some confidence. You're a strong, independent being and you deserve to have a great job and great life. It's like my mentors, Ben and Jerry, once said: If it's not fun, why do it? And they were right.

Create the job you want, pitch it to them, and they'll probably go for it. Who the hell wants a job that has a one-word description? That sounds horrible. You know what some jobs are that have one-word descriptions? Garbageman. Nazi.

If you're not into the whole tech thing, I totally get it. It's really not for everybody. But don't feel sad. That doesn't mean you can't just make up a job. Because, trust me, you still can. Be an entrepreneur and think of something that doesn't exist. Then create that thing. For example: dog

monocles. No one, and I mean no one, has done
that yet. But if marketed correctly you could
definitely get rich owning that space. There are
stupid people everywhere, and if they think it's
cool to buy their dog a monocle, then they will
*definitely* buy their dog a monocle. And if you don't go out
there and create a dog monocle company, I guarantee that
someone else will. It can be whatever your passion is. Find a
space that no one has entered yet and create a need for your
product or restaurant or workout technique. Follow your
heart. Follow your dreams. You can achieve anything that
you set your mind to, and it will take you on the journey of
a lifetime.

    Look at me. I'm the unofficial poster child for Internet
fame. I just did what my heart told me to do and I ended
up here, in front of all of you, so I know that following my
dreams was the right thing to do. Yes, most people over fifty
don't understand what I do for a living or take me seriously,
but does that really matter? They are all going to be retired
or dead soon, and they won't be able to say shit about the
way the world is run. My father can't comprehend that I get
paid to do what I do. He was legitimately shocked when I
told him that I was going to be speaking here today. Trying
to explain to him what I do for a living is what I imagine
it would be like to explain to a father in 1880 that your
job is to "drive a flying machine." He wouldn't be able to

comprehend the notion of being a pilot, in the same way that my dad can't understand how you can be a celebrity for being on the Internet. It's just out of the realm of understanding for someone of that generation.

But the reality is that this is where we are today. So get out there, follow your passion, live your fucking dreams like Martin Luther King Jr., and don't listen to anybody who tells you otherwise. And if you want to get a job with a one-word title, then great! That's fine, too. Some people are into that boring stuff, and that's fine. You will get no judgments from me. I mean, I do tons of wild stuff for my job that I'm sure lots of people judge. Do you. Do what works.

In closing, I'd like to tell all of you that the next few years of your life may seem horrible to you. And compared to the past four years, that may be true. But you have to work to make life fun. You have to try your best to make your dreams come true!!

*(Rip open graduation gown, releasing many doves, drop microphone, get on a horse, ride horse into the open door of a helicopter that is standing by just off stage. As the helicopter takes off and flies over the grads, drop little cute puppies with tiny graduation caps and parachutes out of the chopper. The sun sets in the background.)*

See, my shit is on point. Anyone interested in booking me can email me at #1SuperAmericanMotivationalSpeaker@FatJew.net.

# 21.
# THE INTERN
# HUNGER GAMES

Whatever I initially turned in a first draft of this book I was fucking stoked. I'd spent months working on this thing, dredging up horrible memories from my past in an effort to entertain you, the reader. I also sacrificed everything I enjoy in my life. Haven't sniffed coke off a stripper's C-section scar in months. Haven't reupholstered any furniture (a secret passion of mine) in what feels like forever. Haven't taken ecstasy and gone to the aquarium since I started writing. My penis hasn't been used in so long that it's collecting dust; if you wanted to give me head, you'd have to blow on it first, like people do when they find extremely old books in movies. So you're welcome. After I sent the draft in, I was overjoyed. I could have ejaculated a rainbow of happiness. I've never worked harder on anything in my life. I'd never worked on anything in my life. I had nothing left to give. I was tapped creatively, but it felt kind of good. I'd spent the last half a year immersed in this book, and the notion of having some space from it was intoxicating.

Massages, Netflix binges, eating entire wheels of brie cheese in a single sitting, mani-pedis—all of these things were in my very near future, and I couldn't have been more happy about it. I just lay on my bed with my dog, Toast, licking my ear over and over again. Sheer bliss. I was in a peaceful place for the first time in weeks. I think I dozed off for a second into a serene slumber of nothingness and no responsibility.

But that feeling of euphoria ended when my phone started ringing. I recognized the number as my publisher, Grand Central. Why were they calling me? How long had I been sleeping? Was this one of those things where you are so spent from working so hard that you basically hibernate for like a few days? Could they have edited the book this quickly? *Where the fuck am I?* So many questions.

I answered the phone quickly and abruptly, in the manner that one can only achieve when they've been startled awake and are trying to pretend that they weren't just sleeping.

"Hello, this is me, how are you?"

"Hey, Jew, it's Maddie."

Maddie is my editor's assistant. She has purple hair and is very alt and fun. But I could sense she was in business mode, and I hated her for it.

"Hey, Maddie, what's up, dude? How's it hangin', bruh?"

I was really overdoing the whole "I'm awake and been awake this whole time" vibe.

"We're good over here. Thanks so much for sending the draft over."

"No problem."

"Super excited to read it, but..."

So many horrible thoughts went through my head in a split second. What could the *but* possibly be? She just said they haven't read it yet. Was I that bad of a writer that they read the first page and were like, *no thanks?*

"But what, Maddie? You're freaking me out right now."

"Sorry, I hate to do this. It's just that contractually you are supposed to deliver us a certain number of words for this book, and there just aren't enough words right now."

"Wait, really?"

"Well, you do have a range, but as of now you are not in said range, technically."

"Well, *fuck*. My bad, dog."

"Yeah. I'm sure these page are amazing. I LOL'd at the TOC."

"Oh shit, that's amazing. What's the TOC?"

"Table of contents."

"Right, right, obviously. So how much more do I need to write?"

"At least another two thousand words."

"Uchhhhhh...I literally hate your guts right now."

"I know. I'm sorry. And we need it by the end of this week."

"Isn't it Thursday today?"

"Yeah...but if we are going to make the dates then we have

to edit the whole book over the weekend and then it goes to production right away."

"Dude, I have a mani-pedi appointment this morning, and I'm supposed to go eat lunch at a new strip club in Brooklyn that apparently has amazing gazpacho."

"You missed your deadline on this draft like three times."

"So this is definitely my fault."

"Yes. Definitely."

I hung up the phone in a state of complete denial. I recorked the bottle of rosé I was sipping and sat on the couch with my head in my hands.

Then, an email popped up on my phone. It was from my intern—let's call him Mike to protect his identity. I've put him through enough. The email subject was "Internship Self-Evaluation."

When I opened the email, I realized that it was *from* Mike, *to* his advisor at NYU. Mike was a junior and an undergrad film major. He must've just copied me on the email so that I could read *his* version of what his life had been like over the past semester, as my intern. I opened the attached Word document containing the evaluation, and my heart swelled with excitement. Also, once I read the first page of the self-evaluation, I knew that I would not be writing one more word of this book. The evaluation would *be* a chapter in my book. Because, honestly, nothing really captures the essence of who I am more than what you are about to read.

# NYU

## INTERN SELF-EVALUATION
## TISCH – NYU

**INTERN'S NAME:** MICHAEL M*****

**MENTOR'S NAME(S):** JOSH "FAT JEW" OSTROVSKY

**DATES OF INTERNSHIP:** 9/08/14–5/05/15

**TOTAL NUMBER OF HOURS COMPLETED:**
Too many to count. A lot. Way more than I thought it was going to be.

**WHAT WERE YOUR ORIGINAL GOALS AND EXPECTATIONS FOR THE INTERNSHIP?**
I knew who the Fat Jew was via social media and Internet videos, and that is
what initially drew me to the job posting. I wanted to learn about using the Internet to reach an audience, and as a film major, I thought this was very appeal-
ing. But my goals and expectations for this internship were pretty much thrown
out the window the moment I arrived for my initial "interview" with Fat Jew,
back in September. I was told to meet him in Central Park, but when I arrived I
realized that there were four other NYU students, all vying for the same job. FJ
was nowhere to be found, but after about fifteen minutes of waiting and hanging
out with the other students, he appeared out of some shrubbery wearing a blue
wig, full makeup, and some sort of futuristic silk kimono. He had definitely
just seen *The Hunger Games*, because that movie had just come out and he
was speaking like Elizabeth Banks does in the film. He told us that we would
"embark on a scavenger hunt to win the majestic prize of an internship with
him, and make our districts proud."
　　The whole feeling in the group quickly went from cordial and friendly to
extremely competitive. *Beat out the others, at any cost possible.* Looking back,
I wanted the internship so bad that I don't regret throwing that girl from South
Carolina into a trash can full of ramen noodles and making her cry.

1.

**SPECIFIC INTERNSHIP TASKS**
**Please list some of the specific tasks assigned during the internship.**

| | Exceeded Expectation | Met Expectation | Needs Improvement |
|---|:---:|:---:|:---:|
| Pick up FJ's onesies from dry cleaner | ☐ | ☒ | ☐ |
| Move his car on alternate side street parking days | ☐ | ☒ | ☐ |
| Sew together a thong made of beef jerky | ☐ | ☐ | ☒ |
| Fill giant bowl with chili for FJ to bathe in for vid shoot | ☐ | ☒ | ☐ |
| Have a Hitler mustache for an entire week | ☐ | ☒ | ☐ |
| Sniff some of FJ's dried semen | ☒ | ☐ | ☐ |
| Learn French in under 12 hours | ☐ | ☒ | ☐ |
| Plan a video shoot for Katie Couric interview | ☐ | ☒ | ☐ |
| Read everything to him, including emails, books, text messages, street signs, menus | ☐ | ☒ | ☐ |

**DO YOU FEEL THAT YOUR INTERNSHIP EXPERIENCE WAS USEFUL AND WORTHWHILE? WHY OR WHY NOT?**

I learned a lot about myself during these past nine months. I learned what I'm comfortable doing and what I'm definitely not comfortable doing. For example, I realized I have no problem handling someone's personal tasks like running errands, picking up packages, walking dogs, etc., especially if the payoff is that I get to go to creative meetings about film and TV projects that I'm interested in.

2.

But I now know that I'm not comfortable lying to people about where my boss is, where he has been, or where he is going. He also made me get my anus bleached, and that wasn't something I would want to partake in again. There is a limit to how far I'll go in order to be a part of something that I deem useful. This was a huge lesson for me. I used to think that I would do anything to be a part of the entertainment industry, but I now realize that my personal happiness is my top priority.

**WHAT WERE THE CHALLENGES OR LIMITATIONS OF THE INTERNSHIP?**
The challenges began and ended with my boss, Fat Jew. He is a nice man. Funny, creative, smart, but with any personal assistant–type work, you are going to see all sides of an individual. Picking up two hundred large fries from McDonald's at three a.m. on a Thursday and delivering to his apartment for a stunt he was filming as a joke with his friends felt like an abuse of power. But the fact that it ended up being a part of a really funny video that he posted on Instagram the following day made it feel more like a worthy cause. This is a gray area for me, but one that I'm getting a little more comfortable being in.

**DID YOU HAVE ADEQUATE TRAINING AND ACCESS TO THE RESOURCES NEEDED TO PERFORM ASSIGNED TASKS?**
No one could be prepared in any way for being this man's intern. The level of debauchery I encountered was always eye opening and very often troubling. NYU does not provide any of the resources that I needed to fulfill the tasks that were asked of me during this year. But in a way that made me think outside the box. I learned how to use creative problem solving almost every time I was with Fat Jew. It was horrendous and enlightening all at once.

**HOW HAS YOUR INTERNSHIP EXPERIENCE INFLUENCED YOUR THINKING AND FUTURE CAREER PLANS?**
I'm thinking about going to dental school.

3.

Pretty fucking killer. Also, I just did a word count on this chapter and I'm still just short of two thousand, so how about this:

| | | |
|---|---|---|
| Boobs | Boobs | Boobs |
| Boobs | Boobs | Boobs |
| Boobs | Boobs | Boobs |
| Boobs | Boobs | Boobs |
| Boobs | Boobs | Boobs |
| Boobs | Boobs | Boobs |
| Boobs | Boobs | Boobs |
| Boobs | Boobs | Boobs |
| Boobs | Boobs | Boobs |
| Boobs | Boobs | Boobs |
| Boobs | Boobs | Boobs |
| Boobs | Boobs | Boobs |
| Boobs | Boobs | Boobs |
| Boobs | Boobs | Boobs |
| Boobs | Boobs | Boobs |
| Boobs | Boobs | Boobs |
| Boobs | Boobs | Boobs |
| Boobs | Boobs | Boobs |
| Boobs | Boobs | Boobs |
| Boobs | Boobs | Boobs |
| Boobs | Boobs | Boobs |
| Boobs | Boobs | Boobs |
| Boobs | Boobs | Boobs |
| Boobs | Boobs | Boobs |

| Boobs | Boobs | Boobs |
|-------|-------|-------|
| Boobs | Boobs | Boobs |
| Boobs | Boobs | Boobs |
| Boobs | Boobs | Boobs |
| Boobs | Boobs | Boobs |
| Boobs | Boobs | Boobs |
| Boobs | Boobs | Boobs |
| Boobs | Boobs | Boobs |
| Boobs | Boobs | Boobs |
| Boobs | Boobs | Boobs |
| Boobs | Boobs | Boobs |
| Boobs | Boobs | Boobs |
| Boobs | Boobs | Boobs |
| Boobs | Boobs | Boobs |
| Boobs | Boobs | Boobs |
| Boobs | Boobs | Boobs |
| Boobs | Boobs | Boobs |
| Boobs | Boobs | Boobs |
| Boobs | Boobs | Boobs |
| Boobs | Boobs | Boobs |
| Boobs | Boobs | Boobs |
| Boobs | Boobs | Boobs |
| Boobs | Boobs | Boobs |
| Boobs | Boobs | Boobs |

| | | |
|---|---|---|
| Boobs | Boobs | Boobs |
| Boobs | Boobs | Boobs |
| Boobs | Boobs | Boobs |
| Boobs | Boobs | Boobs |
| Boobs | Boobs | Boobs |
| Boobs | Boobs | Boobs |
| Boobs | Boobs | Boobs |
| Boobs | Boobs | Boobs |
| Boobs | Boobs | Boobs |
| Boobs | Boobs | Boobs |
| Boobs | Boobs | Boobs |
| Boobs | Boobs | Boobs |
| Boobs | Boobs | Boobs |
| Boobs | Boobs | Boobs |
| Boobs | Boobs | Boobs |
| Boobs | Boobs | Boobs |
| Boobs | Boobs | Boobs |
| Boobs | Boobs | Boobs |
| Boobs | Boobs | Boobs |
| Boobs | Boobs | Boobs |
| Boobs | Boobs | Boobs |
| Boobs | Boobs | Boobs |
| Boobs | Boobs | Boobs |
| Boobs | Boobs | Boobs |
| Boobs | Boobs | Boobs |

249

JOSH "THE FAT JEW" OSTROVSKY

| Boobs | Boobs | Boobs |
|-------|-------|-------|
| Boobs | Boobs | Boobs |
| Boobs | Boobs | Boobs |
| Boobs | Boobs | Boobs |
| Boobs | Boobs | Boobs |
| Boobs | Boobs | Boobs |
| Boobs | Boobs | Boobs |
| Boobs | Boobs | Boobs |
| Boobs | Boobs | Boobs |
| Boobs | Boobs | Boobs |
| Boobs | Boobs | Boobs |
| Boobs | Boobs | Boobs |
| Boobs | Boobs | Boobs |
| Boobs | Boobs | Boobs |
| Boobs | Boobs | Boobs |
| Boobs | Boobs | Boobs |
| Boobs | Boobs | Boobs |
| Boobs | Boobs | Boobs |
| Boobs | Boobs | Boobs |
| Boobs | Boobs | Boobs |
| Boobs | Boobs | Boobs |
| Boobs | Boobs | Boobs |
| Boobs | Boobs | Boobs |
| Boobs | Boobs | Boobs |

# APOLOGMENTS

Apparently this is the part where I'm supposed to acknowledge all the people that have helped me with this book and to thank those that have helped to get to where I am in my life. I'm not exactly sure. I wish that I could say what rappers and athletes do regarding their success, something like *"Nobody gave me anything, I put this shit on my back and made it happen! Alone! Like a man!"* but that would be the world's greatest lie. There have been so many people who have helped make this shitshow real. But before we get to that, I think it probably makes more sense for me to take this opportunity to apologize to the people in my life for all of the horrible things I've done to them since I was born. So that's what I'm going to do. It's apologies and acknowledgments all rolled into one, so yes, Apologments.

JOHN MAYER: Sorry I showed up that time I was supposed to interview you for the E! Channel wearing a woman's kimono and Daisy Duke booty shorts. I was only trying to impress you, and I didn't mean to scare you off. Maybe I can interview you sometime in the future?

JANEANE GAROFALO: I'm sorry that I posted your phone number on Twitter and then thousands of teens called you and you had to change your number. Furthermore, I'm sorry that when you saw me on the street in the West Village and screamed at me I told you that you were about as funny as a terrible orphanage fire.

WINONA RYDER: Sorry I stole your number from a model's phone and then texted you a couple harmless photos of my nipples with tiny pepperonis drawn on them so they looked like little pizzas. I'm also sorry that I then tweeted the number out to the world. I did it out of love, obviously. I wanted you to feel the support from your fans that I thought you deserved. Little Winona, you've been through some rough times over the past ten years and I only wanted to help. In all fairness I did get kicked off of Twitter for posting your phone number.

LIL WAYNE: Sorry for running up to you in a Las Vegas casino lobby screaming "Whoopi Goldberg! Whoopi Goldberg! I'm your biggest fan!" and begging for your autograph, thus forcing your security guard to choke me. I knew the whole time that you were not in fact Whoopi Goldberg (although the resemblance is quite striking), and I'm sorry.

P. DIDDY: Sorry for outing you as a homosexual. I'm pretty sure you are, but I'm sorry.

REAL HOUSEWIFE OF NEW YORK KELLY BENSIMON: Sorry for stealing your dirty underpants out of your hamper at your house when you so kindly invited me to your cocktail party. They are now hanging in my den, like the head of an elk.

MOM and DAD: I'm not sure what I have to apologize to you for? Ohhhh, wait—that's right, for soiling the name and reputation that you spent your entire lives building!

EVERY GIRL I'VE EVER HAD SEX WITH: You know that noise I make while ejaculating? I'm sorry for that.

ANYONE WHO WAS THERE THAT ONE NIGHT I GOT DRUNK AND DID THE BORAT VOICE: You know who you are, and I regret doing that every single day of my life and will continue to forever. I was very, very, very drunk, but that is no excuse.

MY BODY: Last but certainly not least, I'm sorry to my body. For drinking bleu cheese dressing out of the bottle with a straw, for getting every tattoo that's ever been suggested to me by an idiotic friend, and for eating six to eight meals a day, like a literal fucking sea lion.

Now for the acknowledgments.

Thank you to David Oliver Cohen, Tainy, Byrd, Ben Greenberg, Bowery Bobby, Gert Jonkers from *Fantastic Man Magazine*, Brittney Crump, rap music (just in general), my shaman Corey, Aaron, Yanina, Rocky Aoki for inventing Benihana, Baby Vinny, Hal Winter, Penelope Ziggy, Miles Berland, Stanley Tucci, Big Veends, Winston Doodooblatt, Alex Ferzan, Mr. and Mrs. Kanye West, Mitchell Charap, KK, Toast, Muppet, Sunshine Sachs, Jason Newman, and a special thank you to January Jones, because without you I could never have written this book. You inspire me daily, and always know the right thing to say.

Moose: we the best

Oh and DOC wants me to thank:

Cristi, Tanner, Maddie Caldwell, CC, Ray Ray and da kids, Uncle Pookie and dem, Marshy, Stew-iana, Jess, Kay Waal, Jason Richman, Caroline Powers, the Internet.

# CREDITS

Comic Book: Brittney Crump

Doddles: Bobby "Bowery Bob" Waltzer

Coloring book: Daniel Amaya

Tyrese and Rashida Jones drawings: Daniel Amaya

Various photos and artwork: Art Direction: Alexander Ferzan

Photo // Image Creation: Justin Waaland, Arizona Kay, Baka

SUPERETTE // superette.nyc

Fat Jew with his book: Guerin Blask

Fat Jew on Balcony with girls: CULPRIT CREATIVE // Pablo Escargot

Fat Jew eating a donut: Peter Svarzbein-www.MongoVision.com
    for *Heeb Magazine* and David Kelsey

Girl Dressed as Fat Jew: Jess Uyeno

Fat Jew wearing Beef Jerky Clothing: Three Jerks LLC and Hagop
    Kalaidijan